The Best Summer of Our Lives

The Best Summer of Our Lives

A photographic history of the
Derbyshire Miners' Holiday Camp

by Geoff Gration

The Breedon Books
Publishing Company
Derby

First published in Great Britain by

The Breedon Books Publishing Company Limited

Breedon House, Unit 3, Parker Centre, Derby DE21 4SZ.

2000

ISBN 1 85983 205 9

Printed and bound by Butler & Tanner Ltd., Selwood Printing
Works, Caxton Road, Frome, Somerset.

Colour separations and jacket printing by GreenShires Group Ltd,
Leicester.

Contents

GEOFF GRATION was born in Derbyshire in 1949. His father, both grandfathers and many of his uncles worked in the Derbyshire pits and, like thousands of others from the local mining community, Geoff's family holidays were spent at the Derbyshire Miners' Holiday Camp at Skegness. When his father died recently, Geoff decided to find out more about the camp. As a result of features which ran in the local press and radio he was inundated with telephone calls, letters and photographs which led to this book. Geoff has spent much of his working life in further education and, with John Titford and John Reilly, he has produced a GCE A level textbook for Communication and Media Studies. He is married with four children.

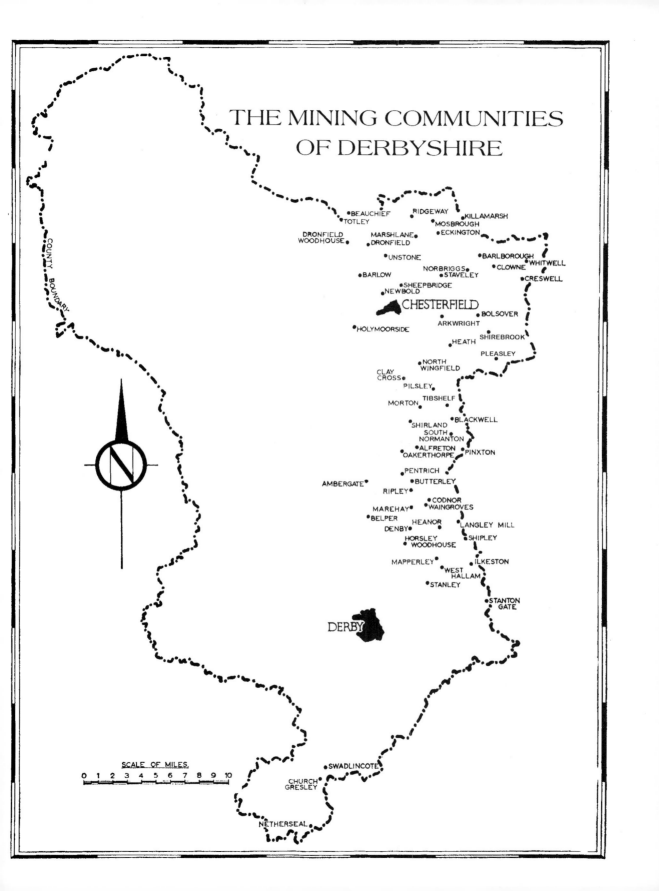

THE MINING COMMUNITIES
OF DERBYSHIRE

Dedicated to my mother and father and the thousands of other Derbyshire mining families who remember their holidays at the Skegness camp with affection and gratitude

Introduction

THE story of the Derbyshire Miners' Holiday Centre is the story of the thousands of mining families who holidayed there and of the people who worked at the camp, many of them from mining families and some ex-miners themselves. It is also the story of the union men who in the 1920s and 1930s fought for a miner's right to take an annual holiday with pay and who made the building of the camp possible. In that sense this is the people's story and in the pages that follow I have tried to tell it by weaving together some of the many photographs and reminiscences made available to me.

I come from one of those thousands of Derbyshire mining families who were able to enjoy, for the first time, a proper holiday by the sea, thanks to the camp at Skegness. When my father, Norman, died recently it brought back memories of happier times at the camp in the 1940s and 1950s. All I could find of this period in the family album were just a few old black and white photographs of the camp and so I decided to try to find out more. As a result of a feature on the camp, which ran in a number of Derbyshire and Skegness newspapers, and on BBC Radio Sheffield and BBC Radio Derby, I was inundated with telephone calls, letters and photographs. It soon became obvious that so many people remembered the camp with great affection and gratitude, and a number of them suggested that a permanent record should be made of those times.

It has not been possible to include in the book all the material made available to me. For example, although the Derbyshire miners also built a similar camp at Rhyl, it seemed appropriate to concentrate on the larger and more popular camp at Skegness. On that basis, I have tried to select those reminiscences and photographs, which best capture the variety of life at the camp, its development and its history. I have also tried to show something of the identity of the old mining community that not long ago stretched along the entire eastern half of Derbyshire where slag heaps and pithead stocks met the eye on nearly every horizon. In the 1940s and 1950s there were some 60 deep coal mines in Derbyshire, employing nearly 50,000 men. At that time Derbyshire mining families accounted for more than a quarter of a million people. Whether it was working down the pits, or playing on the slag heaps and in the pit ponds, the memories of so many people have been coloured by coal. Listening to

'Pilsley Pit always went to camp with Parkhouse Pit and those miners and their families were wonderful people. In those first few years after the war everything was very basic at the camp, but the friendship, the happiness and the memories will stay in our hearts forever, it will always be a talking point wherever we go. Most of all I remember going to the camp in 1947, it was just after the war, I was 14 and it was the best summer of my life.'

Enid White of Pilsley (father Matthew Allsop).

The once familiar face of a miner emerging from underground for a much-needed fag. This is Les Bridges of Ripley, who was a workmate and friend of the author's father.

people's stories was always interesting, whether it involved hearing about the camaraderie of life underground or of the simple, reassuring routine of village life, or of the sense of fun and friendship at the camp. People's stories were often funny, sometimes moving and sometimes sad but invariably it was the sense of family, friendship and community which came across so loud and clear. In the pages that follow I hope I have captured these emotions and this sense of belonging.

I apologise to those individuals who contacted me but who, because of pressure of time, I was unable to visit. With access to so much fascinating material, including over 3,000 photographs, the problem I faced was not so much what to put in the book but what to leave out. Inevitably, some may be disappointed that their favourite photograph does not appear and I apologise for that too. I must also apologise for any inaccuracies there may be with identifying people and with the spelling of names. I have been fortunate enough to be able to rely upon the excellent memories of many people but, inevitably with such a project, there may be some inaccuracies.

There are so many I must thank for their contribution to this book, particularly Avis Millington and Shirley and Harvey Mellors who were able to provide so much useful information and help. Others who contributed material include: Jean Adams, Brian Ashley, Christine Bacon, Frank Bacon, Steve Barnet, Audrey Birks, Malcolm Bond, Vall Bowmer, Doreen Brooker, John Brown, Sally and Harry Burns, John Caulton, Kath Cook, Janet Coope, Gary and Freda Cooper, Mary Cresswell, Rex Darricott, Mrs M. Davies, Dave Eyley, Mrs Eyre, Mr and Mrs Farmer, Len Glenn, Margaret Gorringe, Fred Grace, Susan Graham-Brown, Brian Gration, Doris Gration, Linda Gration, John Gration, Kevin and Jennifer Harris, Ray and Margaret Harris, George Holmes, Denise Howitt, Margaret Hunt, Kitty Jepson, Evelyn Jones, Jim and Winifred Leighton, Stan Longmate, Mrs Eileen Love, Margaret Lyley, Margaret Lyon, Ray and Janet Madely, Margaret Mansell, Kathleen Marsden, Joan McPherson, Deborah Mee, Alan Millband, Joyce and Harry Morris, Kevin Neale, Ben Nolan, Margaret Parkin, Derek Pell, Vondra Redfern, Margaret Scott, Kath and Ivan Slaney, Mr A. E. Smith, Janet Spencer, Colin and Brenda Stone, Eric Taylor, Mr and Mrs Taylor, Sandra Turner, Mary Whetstone, Enid White and Janet Wright. Also I must thank John Shawcroft of the *Ripley and Heanor News*, David Hopkinson of the *Derbyshire Times*, Sarah Winstanley of the *Skegness News*, John Cowpe of the *Skegness Standard*, John Holmes of BBC Radio Derby, Philo Holland of BBC Radio Sheffield and the Local Studies section of Chesterfield Library and Skegness Library.

A Brief History of the Camp

The fight for an annual holiday with pay

It seems incredible that not long after it was considered 'absurd' even to think of time off with pay, that the mining community would build an entire holiday camp by the sea for miners and their families. On the 20 May 1939 the Derbyshire Miners' Holiday Centre at Skegness was officially opened. At the opening ceremony Sir Frederick Sykes, the Chairman of the Miners' Central Welfare Committee said: "I do not think there is any other non-profit making camp of the kind in the country. It is a pioneer venture which is being watched with close interest."

The camp was part of a broader package of welfare and holiday rights won by a long campaign for improved conditions, fought by the Derbyshire Miners' Association before the nationalisation of the coal industry in 1947 and the creation of a single national miners' union. In 1925 the Derbyshire Miners' Association bought nine acres of land at Winthorpe in Skegness for the purpose of building a miners' convalescent home overlooking the sea and with direct access to the beach. The 'Con Home', as it was called by the miners, was opened in 1928 accommodating 120 men and 30 women. Prior to that convalescence for Derbyshire miners was provided in rented accommodation in Skegness. The funds for the purchase of the site were raised by the local union branch committees from galas and dances. Part of the cost of the building of the home was met by a contribution from the Miners' Welfare Fund.

Eventually, the Association succeeded in its campaign for miners to

'Could anything be more absurd in these terribly difficult days than the proposal to grant a fortnight's holiday with full pay?'
A Derbyshire coal-owner commenting in the *Derbyshire Times* in 1922.

have guaranteed time off for an annual holiday with money to spend. In 1936 a Holiday Savings Scheme started which enabled Derbyshire pits to close for a week in the summer with a guaranteed payment to each miner. Most of the holiday money was contributed by the men as savings from their pay with the colliery owners providing a smaller contribution. The building of the holiday camp at Skegness was part of this overall scheme and it was made possible by a donation of £40,000 from the Miners' Welfare Fund and various contributions from the coal-owners. It was capable of accommodating nearly a thousand visitors each week. A miner and his wife were able to have a week's holiday at the camp for £1 and 13 shillings and children over four years of age would each cost an extra 8 shillings and 6d. At this time the savings scheme provided £4 to a married man, £3 to a single man over 18 and £1 and 10 shillings to single men under 18 years of age. Special arrangements were made with the railway companies for cheap fares from Derbyshire to Skegness, and with meals provided at the camp the savings scheme enabled mining families to have a decent holiday away from the pit towns and villages of Derbyshire, often for the first time.

Harry Hicken and the building of the camp

Harry Hicken, union leader and driving force behind the building of the camp, speaking at its opening in May 1939.

Both the savings scheme and the building of the holiday camp at Skegness owed much to the inspiration of Harry Hicken, Derbyshire miner and union man. Harry left school at the age of 12 to work underground at Pilsley colliery as a pony lad earning 10d a shift, or just 4p in new money. In 1912 he was elected checkweighman at Williamthorpe Colliery and became Secretary of the Williamthorpe branch of the Derbyshire Miners' Association. Later, Harry was elected to the National Executive of the Miners' Federation of Great Britain, the forerunner of the National Union of Mineworkers (NUM). In 1942 he joined the Ministry of Fuel and Power and when the Industry was nationalised in 1947 he became Labour Director of the East Midlands Division of the National Coal Board (NCB). During his early years as a miner and miners' leader, Harry Hicken also ran an average of six study groups a week as well as being an outstanding methodist lay preacher. It's not surprising then that a man with such strong principles was a driving force behind the building of the camp. Harry would have seen the first seaside holiday camp, built by Billy Butlin in Skegness in 1936, and thought that the hard-working miners of Derbyshire deserved nothing less than this. Nothing less that is, except for a pub in the camp and strong drink! Harry was a strict methodist teetotaller and he made sure during the early years that no alcohol could be bought at the camp. As well as a committed methodist Harry was also a man of strong socialist principles. It is said that all his life he refused to wear a tie as a mark of his socialism, even when he was appointed to the Ministry of Fuel and Power and to the National Coal Board. In the photograph of the official opening of the camp in 1939, and in the photograph of the opening of the camp's new theatre complex in 1951, Harry is easily distinguishable by this mark of defiance.

In the winter and spring of 1939 men from Vic Hallam Ltd built the camp with the aid of wooden panels pre-fabricated at the company's site in Heanor, Derbyshire. Initially the camp consisted of some 73 large wooden chalets each divided into four separate rooms providing basic sleeping accommodation for four married couples. Flanking the married couples' chalets were rows of 115 so-called 'cubicles' for teenagers and single adults. Along the sea front were a series of large communal wooden buildings housing a children's theatre, lounge and billiards room. Young children were accommodated in a communal dormitory, originally a wooden building overlooking the sea front, and then later replaced by a brick block. Just behind the main entrance to the camp was the largest wooden building of all, which housed the main reception area, dining hall and concert hall. The facilities at this time would be described by us now as 'basic', though Mr Joseph Lynch, the then secretary to the Derbyshire Miners' Association, provides us with this wonderful description of a chalet in the *Derbyshire Times* from 12 May 1939. 'There is provided a double bed which during the daytime may be folded back to the wall and obscured by a curtain, leaving a spacious sitting-room with two chairs and a table. A built-in wardrobe is provided and a wash bowl with water laid on. The floor is covered by a central carpet. The window and bed curtains and bedspread are being merged in a general colour scheme for each chalet expressive of the holiday spirit.' Each chalet was also provided with a large enamel jug to enable hot water to be collected from the hot water points which, like the toilets, were outside and few and far between. Audrey Birks of Old Tupton remembers her father Viron Levers, NUM General Secretary at Williamthorpe Colliery, going early each morning with the white enamel jug for hot water.

In 1939 the camp accommodated 900 visitors a week with each Derbyshire pit taking its turn throughout the season. Unfortunately, those mining families who were scheduled to visit in September of that

'During the war – I must have been six or seven – I went to visit the camp with my Dad. He was a union man and I think he was sent to keep an eye on things when the army had taken it over. I remember he wasn't very pleased when he found some of the soldiers had been using the chalets for bayonet practice!'

John Caulton of Ripley.

'The camp was in a hell of a state after the war. We had to rip out most of the panelling in the chalets. I can remember finding bullets and love letters stuffed behind the walls!'

Frank Bacon of Heanor, who worked for Vic Hallam on the refurbishment of the camp after it was returned to the miners after the war.

The new theatre being opened by Viscount Lord Hyndley in 1951. Note Harry Hicken in the background with his distinctive collar and no tie!

year had to wait seven more years for their holiday at the camp. With the outbreak of war the camp was commandeered by the army for the training of recruits and it wasn't until 1946 that it was handed back to the miners. The young army recruits were not exactly the perfect guests. John Caulton of Ripley remembers his coalminer father threatening to take matters into his own hands when he came across a young recruit using a chalet door for bayonet practice. It took some time after the war for Vic Hallam's to put the camp back into shape. Heanor man, Frank Bacon, who worked for Vic Hallam on the refurbishment, remembers having to replace most of the internal walls of the chalets and finding love letters and bullets stuffed behind the panelling. When the camp returned to full operation after the war each pit was allocated a week on a rota that moved through the season year and year about, so that in the long run each pit had an equal chance of the good weather.

The development of the camp

In 1949 fire destroyed the dining hall, kitchens and concert hall, though most of the other buildings survived, including the chalets. Jean Ellis, the General Manager's secretary, remembers the 'great fire' and drinking ice cold milk recovered from the cold room which, somehow, had survived the flames. By this time the mines had been nationalised and the camp was run by a management committee of trustees drawn from the North Derbyshire branch of the NUM and from the East Midlands Regional Board of the NCB. Harry Hicken's influence had now been overshadowed by that of union leader Bert Wynn who persuaded the trustees, despite objections from Harry, to seek an alcohol sales licence for the camp. Not surprising then that the new theatre and administration complex, built in 1950 of steel and brick to replace and improve upon the facilities destroyed by the fire, contained several bars. The new facilities were opened in July 1951 by Viscount Lord Hyndley at an official opening ceremony followed by a grand reception in the new theatre. A great deal of champagne had been reserved for the dignitaries at the official opening. Shirley Crook worked in the camp's finance department as a teenager in the 1950s and she remembers that most of the staff managed to sample the champagne that day, poured from pot jugs and drunk from tea cups! Eventually the camp would boast some half a dozen bars, most of them in the new complex, making generous profits and helping to keep the camp fees down.

In the early spring of 1953 raging seas brought widespread flooding and devastation to many parts of the Lincolnshire coast, including Skegness. Fortunately, there was little damage to the camp buildings thanks mainly to the sandbag walls hastily constructed by the miners bussed in overnight from Derbyshire. Warnings were given on Friday evening and by Saturday the North Derbyshire NUM Treasurer, Herbert Dilks, had organised busloads of more than 100 men from the three Markham Collieries to help save the camp. Jean Ellis remembers the part the camp staff played that fateful evening, as they received and gave shelter to the homeless from the more devastated parts of Skegness. Another historic event remembered by many staff was the arrival at the camp of refugees, following the Hungarian uprising in 1956. By Christmas of that year the camp housed around 900 male refugees, many of them recruited in Vienna by the NCB for the 'princely sum' of £8 and 6d per week. That year the staff teased each other that they were fully booked by Christmas! Jean Ellis remembers Christmas Day lunch at the camp in 1956 being a very moving occasion as the refugees rose to their feet, en masse, to sing the Hungarian National Anthem.

In the early 1950s a purpose-built block was constructed in brick next to the old Con Home to provide facilities for the many paraplegic miners who had been injured underground. Len Glen of Loscoe, near Heanor, was permanently disabled by a roof fall at Ormonde pit in 1958 and he can remember that in the 1960s and 1970s he had 8, or more, paraplegic mates living close by in the Heanor area. Paraplegic miner Gary Cooper of Riddings, who 'got done' in 1956 at Swanwick pit, told me of a group of Nottinghamshire paraplegic miner friends who used their 'compen' – compensation money – to buy houses on the same street, affectionately known by the locals as 'Para Row'. The camp's Paraplegic Block, or Para Block as it was called, was itself replaced by improved facilities for paraplegic miners in the 1970s. During the 1950s and 1960s all the original wooden structures throughout the whole camp were gradually replaced by brick buildings as new facilities and features were added. In 1960 an open-air heated swimming pool was built and later an indoor heated swimming pool, sauna and health facilities were added. Eventually, additional land was purchased for providing more car parking and sports facilities. In 1975 a new building complex consisting of the Drifters Club, supermarket, amusement arcade, disco and snack bar was opened by Lawrence Daley, General Secretary of the NUM. The following year saw the addition of a complex of self-catering flats, opened by Joe Gormley, President of the NUM.

'There used to be a lot of paraplegic miners a few years ago. Just around Heanor I remember Vin Doggart, Henry Knighton, Bill Burrows, Clarence Priestley, Ken Johnson, Dick Hutchinson. We used to see a lot of each other but there's not many of us left now.'

Len Glen of Loscoe, Heanor, who worked at Ormonde pit until his accident in 1958.

Family fun and entertainment

Throughout its 50 years the emphasis at the Derbyshire Miners' Holiday Centre was on family fun and entertainment. Harold and Sally Burns of Heanor remember that in the early years, up to 1949, sporting competitions and other activities were organised by the union men from each pit. Jack Webster, a Skegness musician, helped provide some entertainment in 1939 and later he was joined by Frank Yexley who acted briefly as the camp's first entertainments manager. Frank was a colourful local publican and boxing promoter who ran the 'Prussian Queen' near Mablethorpe. It seems that Frank had an eye on every chance. George Holmes of Clay Cross remembers playing in a miners versus staff football match at the camp, with Frank acting as referee and as bookmaker. Convinced that they were going to win, the miners placed their bets with Frank only to find that he began to disallow their goals. Apparently, the match ended in some disarray with the miners threatening to throw Frank into the sea! Frank can be seen on many of the early photographs, usually out of doors at this stage, officiating at glamorous grandma and other competitions.

In 1949 there was a young Nottingham-born musician by the name of Mick Millington who was singing in the evenings in pubs in the Skegness area. Frank Yexley asked Mick and his wife Avis, also originally from Nottingham, to join him at the camp to help out, and the rest, as they say, is history. Mick soon established himself as a leading personality at the camp organising and performing much of the entertainment, on and off stage. Out of season he would travel around the Miners' Welfare organisations in Derbyshire providing entertainment, and in the early years could also be seen lending a hand at site maintenance. It wasn't long before Mick was made entertainments manager at the camp, a position he enjoyed right up to the camp's closure in the early 1990s. Avis also worked at the camp and later their two children, Martin and Georgina, also contributed to the entertainment before establishing their own careers in the entertainment and leisure industry elsewhere. Joyce Morris of Poolsbrook near Chesterfield, describes Mick and Avis as 'Mr and Mrs Derbyshire Miners' Holiday Camp' and it's certainly true that in their 40 years at the camp Mick and Avis are remembered with great affection by thousands of Derbyshire mining families. Sadly Mick died in 1996 though Avis still lives in Skegness to this day, at Winthorpe, just a stone's throw away from the Con Home and the site of the old camp.

The Grand Finals weekend at the camp became a special attraction and the results were faithfully reported each year in the *Derbyshire Times*.

'*Mick and Avis Millington were like 'Mr and Mrs Derbyshire Miners' Holiday Camp'.*'

Joyce Morris of Poolsbrook, near Chesterfield.

Avis remembers that in the 1940s and 1950s much of the entertainment involved a high degree of family and audience participation. Almost every conceivable aspect of family and camp life provided an excuse for some activity or other, from 'treasure hunts' in the sand to seeing who could sit on stage the longest without laughing! My favourite was the competition to see who could sew the quickest and neatest patch on someone's backside! Winifred Bennet of Alfreton remembers winning this particular contest in 1947 with family friend Sib Dennis lying across her knees. For some of the higher profile competitions, such as the Ideal Holiday Girl and the Adult Talent Contest, there were the end of season finals for the winners of each particular week. The Grand Finals Weekend, as it was called, developed into a special attraction for the campers and the results of the finals were faithfully reported each year in the *Derbyshire Times*. As well as the finals, there were special holiday weeks at the beginning and end of each season for disabled people and special weekends for the St John's Ambulance Brigade. As Rex Darricott of Duckmanton recalls, the St John's Ambulance Brigade was particularly strong in the Derbyshire mining community where the ever present possibility of accident and death underground bred a respect for the movement. Many mining families were involved in some way with the Brigade and the evening education classes for St John's cadets, and other events and activities, were another strand of community life which has all but disappeared with the closure of the pits.

As the camp became a more sophisticated operation, and as the entertainment began to reflect the trends seen in the development of television and other electronic media, more and more professional acts began to appear on stage. In 1957 new ballroom and theatre facilities were developed and later the 'Golden Butterfly' ballroom and cabaret was developed within the Con Home. The roll call of entertainers is endless but includes Mick Millington, Nobby Clarke, Nick Bernard, Vandra Drew, Pat 'Ginger' Bowman, Big Jack Simpson, Eddie and Pauline, The Smith Brothers and Eric Martin. Eventually, even 'bigger' names were added such as Mike and Bernie Winters, Rosemary Squires, Tony Melody, Cy Grant, Lance Percival, Donald Peers, Kenny Ball and Tommy Cooper. However, no account of the camp entertainment could be complete without mentioning the names of Brian the Singing Miner and his backing group The Flying Pit Props. Brian Ashley worked in the North Derbyshire pits where his impromptu singing sessions in the pithead baths are fondly recalled by Harry Morris of Poolsbrook and

Tommy Cooper outside the Golden Butterfly ballroom with Mick Millington.

many others from the Derbyshire mining community. On holiday at the camp, Brian regularly entered the adult talent competitions and with the support of his friends he invariably brought the house down. It wasn't long before Brian's unique singing voice earned him a recording contract and a big reputation in the pubs and Miners' Welfares in Derbyshire. Together with his backing group The Flying Pit Props, Brian released a cover version of Spanish Eyes and occasionally he can still be heard turning out the odd song at his local pub in Chesterfield.

The camp staff and the photographers

The family atmosphere of the camp, particularly of the early years, was not only evident amongst the campers, but also amongst many of the staff. Shirley Crook recalls that many of the staff were related and many were ex-miners themselves, or came from mining families. Mr A. E. Smith of Stonebroom worked at pits in the Alfreton area, as did his father, brothers and brothers-in-law. In the summer of 1949 he worked at the camp as a waiter where he met his wife-to-be. Doreen Allsop of Pilsley and Joan Clarke of Ripley, also from Derbyshire mining families, worked at the camp as waitresses. One year there were no fewer than seven members from the same mining family working at the camp. Doris Eames (who became Head Housekeeper), her husband Fred (maintenance), her sister Dora McGowan (children's dormitory Matron), Dora's husband Alf (maintenance), Doris and Dora's brother George Wilkinson (maintenance and bars), George's wife Dot (children's dormitory), and for one season only George's father Mr Wilkinson Senior! Most of Doris Eames' extended family worked at the camp for many years and her daughter Vall grew up there. Now Vall Bowmer, and better known to campers as 'Big Vall', she eventually became Head Housekeeper herself, and to this day still works at Skegness Sands on the site of the old camp. Shirley Crook also recalls that the camp was a wonderful place to work. For many years the camp's general manager was Jack Dennis Williamson, better known as 'J. D.' Generally regarded as a good manager, J. D. allowed people to get on with their jobs and only interfered when necessary. As Shirley says, there was no clocking on and off, but by the same token if a job wasn't finished people would stay until it got done.

The work of the camp photographers deserves a special mention because it is thanks to them that we have such a rich and powerful photographic record of the camp and camp life. Nearly all of the

Harvey Mellors and Peter Nolan, two of the camp's photographers with one of their early photo tricks.

thousands of photographs that have survived, of the camp, of the families who stayed there and of the staff, were taken by the photographers employed by the camp. As Dave Eyley, originally of Blackwell, said to me, the typical Derbyshire mining family had about as much chance in the 1940s and 1950s of owning a camera as they did their own car. The only photographic record that most Derbyshire mining families will have of their early personal histories will probably be the occasional official wedding photograph and photographs from the camp. Shirley Crook met her husband-to-be, Harvey Mellors, when he was working at the camp as a photographer. Without the 'shutter bugs', as Harvey described himself, this record of an important part of the Derbyshire mining community would not have been possible.

Fond memories and farewells

Throughout the 1970s and 1980s the camp continued to attract thousands of holidaymakers from the mining communities each season. By now the relative decline of the Derbyshire mining industry, and the rise of affordable alternative holidays, mostly abroad, resulted in the camp opening its doors to mining families from all the British coalfields. One interesting example of the changing aspirations of holidaymakers from the mining community was the Derbyshire Miners' Italian Holiday Scheme, developed by the Derbyshire Area NUM in the 1960s and 1970s. An NUM advertisement from the period proudly boasts of 'Holidays on the sunny Italian Riviera for Miners and their friends at Riccionne on the beautiful Italian Adriatic coast. All-in price 46 guineas for 15 days, air flights and transport from Derbyshire to the airport included.'

Advert from the 1963 Camp Entertainment Programme promoting holidays for Derbyshire miners on the Adriatic.

The camp continued to be owned and run by the Derbyshire Miners' Welfare Centre trustees until 1989. Sadly, the demise of the whole of the British mining industry, and the continued growth of cheap holidays abroad, resulted in all of the assets except the Con Home being sold to private business. In 1990 the camp changed its name to Skegness Sands Holiday Village and continued to function as a holiday centre for a few more years changing hands again in the process. Eventually the current owner of the site, Gordon Hawkins, demolished virtually all of the buildings, with the main exception of the indoor heated swimming pool, and created a static caravan site. The Con Home still stands in all its glory and functions as a convalescent home run by CISWO, the Coal Industries Social Welfare Organisation. Next door, on the site of the old camp, stands nine acres of static caravans directly overlooking the sea, and described by some ex-miners as 'millionaires' row' due to the high annual rents.

Throughout its history the Derbyshire Miners' Holiday Centre provided generations of mining families with their first 'proper holiday' and many deep and abiding memories. For Enid White of Pilsley it provided in 1947 the best summer of her life, the war was finally over and she was a young woman by the sea at last! Ray Madely, originally from Loscoe, appeared on the front of the 1947 August edition of the NCB's magazine Coal News, sitting as a young boy next to his mam and dad on the Skegness beach. Later Ray was able to take his own children for holidays at the camp. I will leave the last word to Janet Wright whose father worked at Renishaw Park pit. In a letter to me Janet wrote: 'Even to this day I still have to have my one day trip to Skeggy each year, though now it is tinged with a little sadness. The 'camp' is no more and so many of my family who helped make those happy holidays are no longer with us. But we have our memories don't we?' Indeed we do Janet, and my hope is that the photographs and reminiscences contained in this book are a fitting record of those times and a fitting tribute to all those who made it possible.

Ray Madely of Langley Mill on the front cover of Coal News with his family at the Skegness camp in 1947.

The Camp

'DERBYSHIRE MINERS' HOLIDAY CENTRE
Opened at Skegness By Sir Frederick Sykes

The holiday centre at Skegness for Derbyshire miners and their families was opened on Saturday by Sir Frederick Sykes, Chairman of the National Miners' Welfare Fund, who described it as a pioneer venture. "I do not think there is any other non-profit making camp of the kind in the country. It is a pioneer venture which is being watched with close interest. When we remember that there are some 3,000,000 people in the mining community who are affected by the holidays with pay scheme this year, we can appreciate the importance of the lead which is being given here today." The main credit for the scheme belongs to Mr H. Hicken, the General Secretary of The Derbyshire Miners' Association, and then to the Derbyshire Miners' Welfare Committee. The cost is about £35,000 and has been provided by a grant from the National Miners' Welfare Fund.'

The *Derbyshire Times*, 26 May 1939.

Harry Hicken, union leader and driving force behind the building of the camp speaking to a group of north Derbyshire miners at the official opening in May 1939. As well as a methodist lay preacher, Harry was also a committed socialist and it is said that all his life he refused to wear a collar and tie as a mark of his socialism.

Opposite, a view towards the sea over the tops of some completed chalets and cubicles, with the lounge and the first children's dormitory still under construction. Later, a brick dormitory was built and the original wooden dormitory was converted into the Jolly Goblin children's theatre.

'Most of the original camp was built of prefabricated wooden panels made at Vic Hallam's first yard at Marlpool, Heanor, before the factory moved to Langley Mill. Vic had teams of men lodging in Skegness erecting the chalets. I was up there myself after the war refurbishing the camp after it was handed back from the military.'

Frank Bacon, of Heanor, who worked for Vic Hallam for many years.

Men from Vic Hallam Ltd of Heanor pose for this picture during tea break in front of the company board. In the background is the tea and sandwich kiosk under construction.

The same kiosk in use some years later.

'MARRIED PEOPLE'S ACCOMMODATION

Each chalet has four separate rooms, one of which will be allotted to each married couple. There is provided a double bed which during the daytime may be folded back to the wall and obscured by a curtain, leaving a spacious sitting room with two chairs and a table. A built-in wardrobe is provided and washbowl with water laid on. The floor is covered with a centre carpet. The window and bed, curtains and bedspread are being merged in a general colour scheme for each chalet, which will be expressive of the holiday spirit. Where the occupants have a child under the age of four years there is provided, free of charge, a fully-equipped cot. The interior walls are reinforced by a composition which renders each room practically soundproof from the others. The charge for this room will be 16 shillings 6d per week.'

The *Derbyshire Times*, 12 May 1939.

Married couples' chalet, number 226 and 227. Having a photograph taken in front of your chalet door was very popular and before 1947, as in this photograph, all the chalets could be seen in their bare wood finish.

A later view of the chalets showing the renovated and painted black and white exteriors.

'SINGLE PERSON'S ACCOMMODATION

This will be in cubicles. Each cubicle contains two single beds which may be folded back during the daytime, the furnishing and decoration being on similar lines to those of the chalets. Where two friends, brothers or sisters are going together, arrangements may be made for them to occupy the same cubicle. The charge per person will be 8 shillings per week.'

The *Derbyshire Times*, 12 May 1939

The rows of 115 so-called 'cubicles' for teenagers and single adults were built flanking the married couples' chalets. The end of the row above also housed a stall selling rock and other fancy goods and led down to the tea and sandwich kiosk.

'CHILDREN'S ACCOMMODATION

The Children's Dormitory will provide sleeping accommodation for children over three and under nine years of age in 100 single beds. Parents will take their children and put them to bed, after which a trained nurse will be in attendance throughout the night to administer to their wants. During the daytime they will accompany their parents in the chalets. There is also provided a well-equipped children's playroom for use in inclement weather. The charge per child will be 4 shillings per week. Children nine years of age and over will be accommodated in the cubicles at a charge of 8 shillings per week.'

The *Derbyshire Times*, 12 May 1939.

The original children's dormitory was located in the wooden building overlooking the sea front which later became the Jolly Goblin theatre. Possibly because of the fear of fire, this more substantial brick dormitory above was constructed near the new theatre complex. Shaped like a giant H, the girls' and boys' blocks were separated by the connecting corridor seen in the above picture.

The rows of empty beds wait for the excited children.

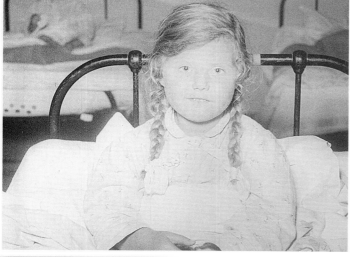

Janet Wrigley – now Janet Wright – is tucked into bed in one of the old iron bedsteads from 1947 or 1948. The camp photographers regularly included the children's dormitory on their rounds and several of these photographs are shown in the next chapter. I remember my first time in the dormitory at the age of three and our next door neighbour, Trevor Hodson, being given strict instructions to look after me!

'PROVISION OF FOOD

When staying in the apartment house the wife has still some of the ordinary household drudgery to perform in buying in her daily supply of food for the family. At the centre she is absolved free from this task, her day of rest and enjoyment begins when she rises. Well-balanced menus will be provided at each meal of the day, at a price calculated to meet the cost of the food and its preparation only. It should be noted that a first-class hotel chef and competent kitchen staff have been engaged and the meals supplied should not suffer by comparison with those of the more expensive hotels. They will be substantial and will be prepared under the most hygienic conditions and with the latest type of equipment procurable. The prices of the meals have not definitely been fixed but it is expected that breakfast will be put on for approximately 6d to 8d; lunch, four-course, approximately 9d to 1 shilling; tea, approximately 6d to 8d. Suppers will be provided and for these the latest type chip-potato range is being installed.'

The *Derbyshire Times*, 12 May 1939

The dining hall and kitchens in the early 1960s. The original kitchens and dining room were built of wood and were destroyed in the great fire of 1949. The theatre built after the great fire, was also used up to 1957 to serve food, particularly for special receptions. In the kitchens Bill Ewles, Head Chef, can be seen at right of picture. Others include: Mrs Shaw, Annie Truswell of Pilsley, and 'little Amy'.

'Viscount Lord Hyndley opened the new theatre complex and a grand meal was served for the dignitaries in the new theatre/ballroom and I remember the champagne flowed! Most of us staff managed to wangle a drink of champagne, poured from pot jugs and drunk from tea cups!'

Shirley Crook, now Shirley Mellors, who worked in the camp's finance department.

This compilation, above and opposite, shows the various stages of construction of the theatre and administration complex built in 1950 and opened in 1951, following the great fire in 1949 when the main wooden buildings at the heart of the camp were destroyed. This new complex was also the first part of a long-term programme of replacing all of the wooden structures with brick buildings. Below left shows Viscount Lord Hyndley, Chairman of the National Coal Board, delivering his address at the official opening. Harry Hicken, the union leader said to be the driving force behind the camp's creation, is second from the right and is easily distinguishable by his continuing refusal to wear a tie, even on this great occasion. Bottom right is the reception Shirley Mellors refers to above, the reception were most of the staff managed to wangle a drink of champagne from tea cups!

'For the start of the season the bathing pool had been completed and this had proved most popular. By next year they should have another block of brick chalets and by the end of three years the conversion to brick chalets should be complete.'

The *Derbyshire Times*, 23 September 1960.

As this compilation of shots from the early 1960s shows, the conversion to brick buildings was now almost complete. In the photograph immediately below, a few of the original wooden chalets remain standing in front of the newly built brick block. The picture opposite shows the open air heated swimming pool opened in 1960 as referred to above.

'*This new building is the latest development and replaces the last of the old wooden structures. The complex comprises 'The Drifters Club', discotheque, coffee bar, amusement arcade, photographic shop, first aid centre, bookmaker's office and supermarket. Landscaping of the new area has been undertaken to provide shelter from the prevailing winds.*'

Souvenir Programme, The Opening Of The New Building Complex, 1975.

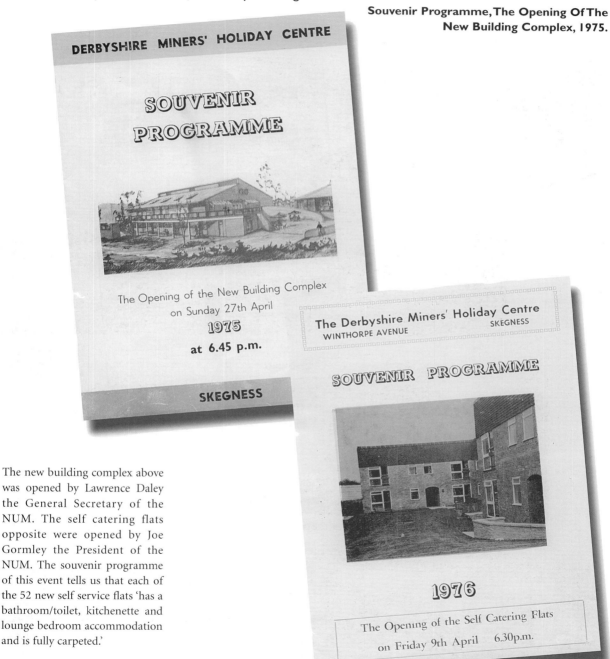

The new building complex above was opened by Lawrence Daley the General Secretary of the NUM. The self catering flats opposite were opened by Joe Gormley the President of the NUM. The souvenir programme of this event tells us that each of the 52 new self service flats 'has a bathroom/toilet, kitchenette and lounge bedroom accommodation and is fully carpeted.'

'The boss — J. D. Williamson — had lots of cronies and always seemed to have a finger in every pie. One of his friends had a light aircraft and J. D. persuaded him to help us with some aerial photographs of the camp which ended up as postcards for sale.'

Harvey Mellors, camp photographer.

The postcard shows the camp as it was originally built in 1939. In the centre foreground is the large wooden dining room/concert hall and administration complex destroyed in the great fire of 1949.

This aerial view was taken in 1963 and shows the theatre complex and convalescent home in the foreground with a combination of the old wooden chalets and new brick chalets in the background.

'With the building of a new ballroom, bars and lounge, and the almost complete reconstruction of the theatre, the Derbyshire Miners' Welfare Holiday Centre at Skegness has some of the most attractive and well-equipped buildings in the whole country.'

The *Derbyshire Times*, 7 June 1957.

This 1950s' aerial photograph shows a good view of the 1957 extension to the theatre complex referred to in the *Derbyshire Times*.

This 1980s' view shows the full and final development of the camp including the new Drifters Club, self-catering flats, and paraplegic facilities.

'It broke my heart when they demolished the camp. I used to go and watch them nearly every day. The lads doing the demolition knew how much it meant to me. The day they knocked down the old theatre they waited for me to arrive before they started.'

Vall Bowmer – 'Big Vall' – who grew up on the camp and worked there most of her life.

These photographs were made available to me by Vall Bowmer who saw it as her duty to record the camp's destruction in the early 1990s. Vall grew up on the camp with her parents Fred and Doris Eames and to this day she works on the site of the old camp at the Skegness Sands caravan park.

'Not that long ago we were in Skegness, so we decided to call in and have a look at the old camp – it was years since we'd been there. But it was all gone, it was just like one big car park, bit sad really. We took some photographs for old times' sake.'

Brenda Stone, of Heanor.

These photographs from Brenda Stone were taken in the early 1990s after the demolition of virtually all of the camp's buildings. The indoor swimming pool survived, as did the building below, and both were incorporated into the Skegness Sands caravan park which now stands on the site.

'Where the camp used to be it's just caravans now, next to the Con Home – that's still there. Mind you, I have to say it's a very nice site – lots of statics overlooking the sea – expensive though. They call it 'Millionaires' Row'!'

Ivan Slaney, of Ilkeston.

The Convalescent Home as it is today, still run by Coal Industries Social Welfare Organisation (CISWO) to provide a restful break for people from mining families. To the right of the Con Home you can just see the area once occupied by the paraplegic block and now part of the Skegness Sands caravan site.

Further to the right of the Con Home and overlooking the sea is 'millionaires' row' referred to above by Ivan Slaney.

The Campers

'Before our pit closed Pilsley was a proper little village with our own railway station. Every year half the village went to the Holiday Camp and the other half went to the station to see us off. Mr Brailsford, a miner himself, had a horse and cart and he took most of the people's luggage to the station and we walked behind. He was there when we came home a week later to bring the luggage back.'

Enid White of Pilsley; both Enid's father and husband worked at Pilsley pit until it closed in 1957.

Most of the mining community of the village of Pilsley at the Skegness camp in 1951. Enid White and her friend Doreen Brooker, then Enid Allsop and Doreen Walters, are the two young women standing at the extreme left of the group.

This photograph shows the Coppice and Woodside pits of Heanor at the camp in 1947. In the centre of the group is Colin Stone as a young boy with glasses, standing between his mother Mary and father Harry. In front of Colin and Mary Stone, kneeling, is Tommy Hunt local councillor and NUM official at Coppice pit. The big man at the extreme left of the group is George Fardon.

'*The houses in Tavistock Square, Alfreton, flank a patch of marshy ground called the green. Once the green was used as a playing field. In summer the people danced on it to records. There existed the warmth and friendliness associated with a mining community. Everyone knew everyone and their common bond was the pit. It affected the life of each of them. The little community has been dying since the source of life – the colliery – was cut off.*'

The *Derbyshire Times,* on the closure of Alfreton pit in 1968.

This photograph above of Alfreton pit was loaned to me by Jim and Winifred Leighton who lived in Tavistock Square for many years and who campaigned against the closure of the pit. As well as Jim and Winifred and their son Victor, the photograph shows Mick Beastall holding the board and John Parker, both also of Tavistock Square.

The Creswell Colliery Welfare Bugle Band, from the village of Creswell at camp in, I believe, the early 1960s.

36

'TRAVELLING

As the result of protracted negotiations with the railway companies, it has been possible to cut down the usual cost of a period ticket very considerably. Trains will be run from most of the stations adjacent to the homes of the people travelling at a cost of 8 shillings 6d for adults and 5 shillings for children not over 14 years of age. Children under 4 will travel free. It will be noted that the saving in railway fare is almost equivalent to the cost of accommodation for the week. On arrival at the Skegness station passengers will be taken in buses to the Centre, and will be brought from the Centre to the station again at the weekend without extra charge.'

The *Derbyshire Times*, 12 May 1939.

These photographs of the train journey to and from Derbyshire were taken by my uncle, Doug Gration, an amateur photographer when he wasn't down the pits. Virtually all of the photographs made available to me were taken at the camp by the camp photographers and these pictures taken by my uncle are the only ones I have seen of the journey to Skegness. Top left is my cousin Derek with family friend Gwen Clarke. Bottom left is me, sitting on the grass without a hat with one of my twin sisters and my cousin Tony waiting to board the train back to Derbyshire.

'The day we'd go to camp I'd wake up in the morning in Blackwell with my brothers, sister and my Mam and Dad, uncles, aunts and cousins and all my mates from the village. And the next day I'd wake up in Skeggy with my brothers, sister and my Mam and Dad, my uncles and aunts and all my mates! It was like the whole village just upped sticks and moved to Skeggy for the week. Every year we went to camp and I just assumed everybody else did. When I was about 13 I overheard a lad on the bus to school saying he was going on holiday to a place called 'Yarmouth'. "Yarmouth? Yarmouth?" I asked, "you mean Skeggy don't you?"'

Dave Eyley, originally from Blackwell, whose father Albert was at Blackwell Pit.

The Eyley family and friends from Blackwell relaxing on the Skegness beach in the early 1960s. Dave Eyley is the young boy in the centre of the picture. Others include: Phyllis Sales, Roy Sales, Albert and Rene Eyley. Dave's father, Albert, worked at the Blackwell pit until it closed in 1970.

To the left of picture, Dave Eyley with his brother in the boys' dormitory at the Skegness camp in the mid-1960s.

'I don't remember that we packed much luggage — certainly not the ritual that it is today — but then again we didn't have many clothes! What I still find strange when I look at all those old photographs is that the men, even on holiday, still wore their long, thick trousers, jackets, caps, fair-isle jumpers, shirts and ties.'

Janet Wrigley, now Janet Wright of Spinkhill near Chesterfield.

Janet Wrigley can be seen helping her Uncle 'Biz' – Bill Fox – in a camp sandcastle competition in the late 1940s. As Janet says, note the tie, waistcoat and watch chain.

This photograph from 1955 shows most of the Clarke family of Ripley on the Skegness beach, dressed to kill! In the centre of the group are Mr and Mrs Clarke, sitting with their daughters Joan, Shirley and Margaret and with young Susan playing in the sand. Standing and suited are Shirley's husband, Alan Anthony, and Margaret's husband, John Hunt; sitting is Joan's husband, Don McPherson.

'There was only cold water in the chalets – no hot water – and no toilets either. I remember my Dad every morning used to get us all a big jug of hot water from the hot water standpipe in the yard.'
Margaret Boulton, now Margaret Mansell of North Wingfield.

One of the hot water standpipes is just out of shot to the right of this early morning scene. Walking away from the standpipe, fag in mouth and jug of hot water in hand, is Mr George Hill of Ripley.

This is the only inside view I have been able to find of the original wooden chalets built for married couples and very young children. On the foldaway bed is my cousin Christine Gration. Note the hot water jug on the side.

'At 6 o'clock in the morning you'd see many of the miners walking around the camp. You see, when you've been doing regular 'earlies' (early morning shift) you just got in the habit of waking up at that time. Most of us would go round to Smokey Joe's café for a proper greasy breakfast.'

Harry Burns, Ripley and Ormonde pits.

Inside Smokey Joe's café. Sitting is an assistant photographer who worked for Frank Richards and standing to the right is, I believe, 'Smokey Joe' himself, Fred Spencer originally of Clay Cross. The café was run by Fred and by Mona Keaton, also originally of Clay Cross.

Tucking into one of Smokey Joe's greasy specials is left, George Bradley and right, George Holmes, both of Parkhouse pit near Clay Cross. George distinctly remembers that this was supper in 1952, and not breakfast!

'All the chalets looked alike and the children were always getting lost amongst them. We bought a flag and windmill to fasten to ours so that the children could find it.'

Mrs M. Davies of Ironville, her husband Jack worked at Alfreton pit for 22 years until he was made redundant in 1969.

Mrs Davies' children letting themselves into their chalet. The children are a little older here, so no need for the windmill to guide them on their way.

A good child's-eye view of an impromptu skiffle session from the early 1950s with the chalets stretching out into the distance towards the Con Home.

'Pilsley Pit always went to camp with Parkhouse Pit and those miners and their families were wonderful people. In those first few years after the war everything was very basic, but the friendship, the happiness and the memories will stay in our hearts forever, it will always be a talking point wherever we go. Most of all I remember going to the camp in 1947, it was just after the war, I was 14 and it was the best summer of my life.'

Enid White, father Matthew Allsop.

Enid is sitting on the wall third from the right with her sister Eileen Allsop, now Lindley, second from the right. Also in the picture from the Pilsley area are Marion Weaver, Doreen Lowbridge, and Pearl and Edna Mason.

To the right in this beach scene is Enid's friend from Pilsley Doreen Walters, now Brooker. Doreen worked at the camp as a waitress. The other young woman is Nancy Limb.

'My Dad was a Pit Deputy, so of course we always went to Butlin's instead.'
Lorraine Greaves, now Lorraine Komorowski of Heanor.

My Dad wasn't a pit Deputy, so of course we didn't go to Butlins! Except, that is, for this one occasion in 1949 above when the family walked across from the miners' camp to visit some friends who were staying at Butlin's. From the left are my father Norman, mother Doris, my Aunts Doreen Wild and Ivy Musgrave and Uncle Cliff Musgrave. Standing are my cousins, from the left John and David Musgrave, Margaret, Neville and Ian Wild. In the pram are my twin sisters Janet and Jennifer.

Twenty years later, my youngest sister, Deborah, made it to the Derbyshire Miners' Holiday camp, seen here between our parents.

'In May 1939 my husband and I spent our honeymoon at the Derbyshire Miners' camp at Winthorpe and 60 years later in May 1999 we celebrated our Diamond anniversary with friends at Winthorpe.'
Sally Burns, whose husband Harry Burns worked at Ripley and Ormonde pits.

Sally and Harry Burns are pictured here on the Skegness beach in 1952 or 1953 with their daughters Brenda and Christine and their son John.

Mr and Mrs Burns with Derbyshire miners' union leader Bert Wynn and his wife Florrie. Taking over from Harry Hicken, Bert played a central role in the development of the camp.

'There's a great photograph of my father, Jim Longmate, with some of his cronies outside the camp a bit of the worse for drink. They'd gone out to Skegness and came back in a taxi. But it was too late, they'd already missed dinner and the wives weren't very pleased, especially my mother. She played piano at the Methodist Chapel and only had one drink a year when she came to camp.'

Stan Longmate of Tibshelf, Stan's father Jim Longmate worked regular nights at Moreton pit.

A good time in the Skegness pubs was obviously had by all, as this picture shows taken on the return to the camp sometime in 1947. Pity about missing dinner though! Jim Longmate is second from the left and Tommy Carr is at the extreme right of picture. All the men in this photograph worked at Bonds Main pit, Temple Normanton, near Chesterfield.

Some 25 years later at the camp, Jim Longmate and his wife, Hilda, relax in the bar. To the left is Jim's son Stanley with his wife, Brenda. To the right is another son, Dennis, and his wife.

'Sometimes the staff might forget to put a chamber pot under the bed in each chalet — remember there were only 2 or 3 lots of outside toilets dotted around the outside of the camp. Wives invariably sent husbands to reception with this request and, I don't know why, they were so embarrassed and referred to the chamber pots as "guzundas" or "them there things as guz under bed"!'

Shirley Crook, now Shirley Mellors, who worked at the camp in the 1950s.

Benny (William) Barker from Blackwell stayed at the miners' Convalescent Home in the late 1930s and can be seen here earning some pocket money helping out with the toilet arrangements at the Con Home. In the background the holiday camp is under construction.

Benny Barker's friends, the Bennett family, play 'Rum-stick-a-bum-finger-or-thumb' at the camp. From the right: John Bennett, Mr Brooks, Lena Kennings, Winifred Bennett, Pauline Kennings, Teresa Bennett, Peter Walker.

'Every year before we went to Camp my mam used to say "I hope it's not same week as Shirebrook – there'll be trouble if it is." They had a bit of a reputation for being a rough lot from Shirebrook.'

Mrs Madely of Langley Mill, her father was 'Cappa' Capewell who worked at Ormonde Pit.

Mr 'Cappa' Capewell and his family at their chalet door. That's Janet Capewell, now Janet Madely, holding on to her mother's dress and sitting next to a family friend. Her brother, Kenneth Capewell, is standing. Of all the photographs I've seen of Cappa, this is the only one where he isn't wearing his cap, though see below.

That's better! Opposite, Cappa Capewell as he should be with his cap, and wife, Gwen, in the camp's Tavern bar in the early 1950s.

'We used to get up to some right tricks at the camp. You'd be on the beach with other families and you might bury a chap's shoes in the sand and wait for him to try and find them! We had some great fun.'

Fred Grace of Waingroves who worked in the pits in the Ripley area for many years and as a pit Deputy. Fred is also a lay preacher and was a local councillor and former Mayor of Ripley.

Fred Grace and his wife, Edna, at right of picture with fellow Ripley miner Jack Wheatley and his wife.

Mrs Taylor of Ripley sitting on a neighbour's knee, with her daughter on the airbed. Although Mr Taylor didn't work down the pits a friend of his – Les Bridges – did and Les acted as a guarantor enabling the Taylor family to holiday at the camp.

'My father was Viron Levers, NUM General Secretary at Williamthorpe pit. Most of the men in our family worked in the pits and we went to the camp each summer for years. We always had the same chalet overlooking the sea front.'

Audrey Levers, now Audrey Birks of Old Tupton.

The Levers family outside their chalet overlooking the sea. Viron Levers is at the left of the picture with his daughter Audrey at the front of the group in the middle. Also in the picture are Viron's wife Edna, daughter Dorothy, sons Cyril and Bryan, and Cyril's wife Cathlene.

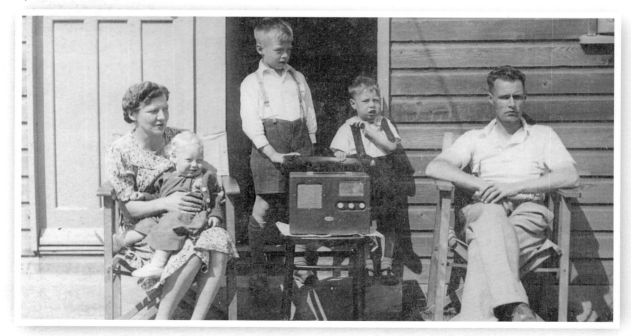

Another family group outside their chalet door, this time my uncle Doug Gration with his wife Bertha and sons Brian, Derek and Tony.

'One year at the camp we ended up on the front cover of the National Coal Board's magazine, Coal News. All his life my dad had a quiff in his hair and you can see it in all the photos. I went to the camp from being a little kid and I ended up taking my own children there.'

Ray Madely, originally of Loscoe, his father Len Madely worked at Ormonde pit.

Ray Madely is the youngest of the Madely family in the photograph opposite, and in the Coal News below. His father's quiff which Ray refers to, is visible in both pictures!

Bottom left shows Ray with his own son at the camp walking up Winthorpe Avenue in the 1970s.

'Many of the people from the camp used to walk past our photographic shop on Seathorne Crescent, just off Roman Bank. Dad had a rocking horse which was usually standing outside and the campers used to sit their children on it to have a photo taken.'

Margaret Gorringe of Northampton – Margaret's father ran 'Frank Richards' photographic shop just a few hundred yards from the camp.

The picture directly above shows Frank Richards' daughter Margaret on the rocking horse when it was new. The other, later shots are of the same horse outside Frank's shop showing it in various states of wear and repair. Clockwise, starting top left, are: Margaret Jackson of Chesterfield; me, aged two or three; Glyn Jones of North Wingfield; Gwen Clarke of Ripley and to the left of the horse is my aunt Bertha Gration.

'I remember the children's parties with the paper hats and lots of jelly and ice cream. Afterwards we'd all parade down to the theatre on the seafront to watch cartoons. Oh yes, and I remember the pillow fights in the dormitory!'

John Tate, originally of Newthorpe, Nottinghamshire, whose father John Tate worked at Moorgreen pit.

From the left are: Gordon Jackson, Malcolm Morley, Bryan Levers and Bill Morley. Bryan's father, Viron Levers, was NUM General Secretary at Williamthorpe pit.

Brothers Roger and John Tate of Newthorpe, left and right, and their cousin Derek Levers in the middle. Notice the rows of metal teapots in the background.

From the left are: Trevor Hodson, my sister Jennifer, me, my sister Janet, and turning away from the camera Vivian Hodson, all from Ripley. The Hodson family were our next door neighbours.

'Wednesday, 4.00pm

Children, it's — PARTY TIME! Party food, Party Panto and Film Funny Cartoons. Don't forget to tell your parents — come along and join the Pied Piper Parade afterwards!'

Camp Entertainment Programme.

Left is Tony Gration, my cousin, and at the right of the picture are his sister and brother Christine and Brian Gration. Their father, Doug, worked at the Ripley pits. The girl in the middle was a family friend.

Second from the left is Jean Calladine of Heanor and her mother, Flo Calladine, is standing behind her. Jean's father, Bill, worked at Ormonde pit.

Second from the right is Melvyn Truswell of Pilsley. I'm not able to name the other boys in the picture but I believe they all came from the Pilsley area.

'After the children's party there'd be a parade with all the children being led out of the dining hall and around the camp by the musicians and entertainers.'

Enid Allsop of Pilsley, now Enid White.

Above, this photograph of the children's parade was loaned to me by Audrey Birks of Old Tupton. In the middle of the group is John Morley, Audrey's cousin, and her brother Bryan Levers. Also in the middle of the group is Gordon Jackson, a family friend. Bryan and Audrey's father was Viron Levers who worked at Williamthorpe pit.

At left of this picture, near the bicycle, are brothers John and Roger Tate in this children's party parade from 1954. In the centre background of this picture you can just see the back legs of Jumbo, the mechanical elephant which 'walked' up and down the sea front at this time.

This photograph of the children's parade was loaned to me by Colin and Brenda Stone of Heanor and it shows Jean Calladine at the right of the second row from the front. Jean's father was Bill Calladine who worked at Ormonde pit.

'I remember the dormitory and the children's matron — she seemed very strict. I remember having to get changed for bed in my parents' chalet and then having to troop across to the dormitory in bright sunshine to go to bed when everybody else seemed be going out for the night. I was 23 when my parents last made me do that — no, only joking!'

Kevin Harris, originally of Alfreton, whose father Ray worked at Pyehill pit.

After the children's party, Margaret Smith of Alfreton with her four cousins, Brenda, Eileen, Marilyn and Andrea Wall. Margaret's father, Arthur Smith, worked at Swanwick pit.

Joan Turner of Arkwright with her cousin Susan Turner to her right. Joan's father, Roland 'Toby' Turner, worked at Arkwright pit and it was in his house that the methane problem was first discovered which led to the eventual demolition and re-siting of the entire village of Arkwright.

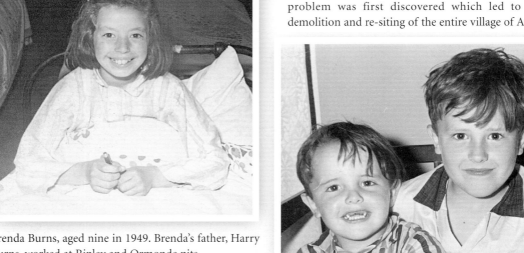

Brenda Burns, aged nine in 1949. Brenda's father, Harry Burns, worked at Ripley and Ormonde pits.

Kevin Harris, at right of picture, in 1964 with his brother David. Their father, Ray Harris, worked at Pyehill pit.

'I went to the camp in the 1960s with my auntie and her family and friends. As a child I slept in the dormitory and when we were all in bed in our pyjamas a photographer came along each row of beds taking pictures. Haven't times changed — would that be allowed now?'

Denise Howitt of Borrowash.

Left is Steve Barnet who now lives at Swanwick and below is his brother. Steve's father was Eric Barnet who worked at Glapwell, Holmewood, Williamthorpe and Ireland pits.

Above, John Mellors and opposite, his sister Hazel Mellors, now Mrs Lait. Both of these photographs were loaned to me by Evelyn Jones of North Wingfield who tells me that John is now the headteacher of a north Derbyshire school.

'My husband Earnest worked at Holmewood pit and then Arkwright pit until it was closed. We'd been going to the camp since the 1940s and when they closed Arkwright pit in the 1980s all the men and their wives got a free holiday at the camp. Most of the people I went with on that free holiday are dead now.'

Evelyn Jones of North Wingfield.

Some of the men and their wives on the free holiday at the camp organised by the NUM after the closure of Arkwright pit in the 1980s. Earnest and Evelyn Jones are second and third from the left; Mr and Mrs Harry Tuck are first and fifth from the left and Mr and Mrs Cotterill are first and second from the right.

Evelyn and Earnest Jones in front of the Drifters bar on the same free holiday organised after the closure of Arkwright pit.

'After a full day on the beach and in the swimming pool the children would be tired out and so we'd be able to enjoy an hour in the evening in the ballroom or in the bar.'

Margaret and Ray Harris of Alfreton; Ray worked at Pyehill pit.

Relaxing in the evening in 1965, from left to right are: Mr and Mrs Frank Tomlinson, Margaret and Ray Harris, Mr and Mrs Brian North.

From left to right: M. Wardale, Ray Hunt, Carol and Barry Hanson, June and John Caulton, Harold and Louie Hillier. In this picture from the mid-1960s, all the men worked at Swanwick pit.

'The first time back at the camp in 1985 after the big strike was one hell of a party. We'd had nothing coming into the house for months, so at the end of it all being at the camp with our friends was a time to let down our hair.'

Joyce Morris of Poolsbrook near Chesterfield; her husband Harry Morris worked mainly at Ireland pit.

The summer of 1985 and party time at the camp after the long, hard miners' strike which started in 1984 and dragged through to the following year. Standing from left: Addie Hudson, Colin Winnard, Keith Williams. Sitting from left: Harry and Joyce Morris, Terry and Cath Hall, Trevor and Lil Wilkinson.

Some years earlier at the camp in the '70s, to the left of this group, is Joyce with her first husband Geoff Evans. Also in the group are Joyce's daughters Margaret and Linda Evans, niece Irene Evans and Pete and Pat Marshall.

'Did you know that Glapwell was the thirstiest colliery in the county? We had the biggest receipts from the bar while they were here, and we have sent a cup to one of their officials in honour of their achievement!'

J. D. Williamson, the camp's General Manager, quoted in the *Derbyshire Times*, 23 September 1949.

From left to right: Arthur Brown, Les Bridges and my father Norman Gration, all from the Ripley and Denby pits. I love the low slung belts in this picture. Under magnification the time on Les's watch is 6.40 – first pint of this night in 1952?

In the theatre enjoying a drink during the performance are George and Ethel Morley. George worked at Williamthorpe pit in the blacksmith's shop.

'I worked at the camp in the summer of 1975, mostly in the bars and restaurants. It was booming then and not just with Derbyshire miners. I remember a rugby league club from Wakefield staying there and nearly drinking us dry.'

Alan Millband, originally from Ripley.

At left of picture are Vera, Bill and Flo Calladine from Heanor. Bill worked at Ormonde pit and his daughter Jean is third from the right.

From left to right: Ivan and Kath Slaney of Ilkeston (Kath's father, Harry Hart, worked at Ormonde and Coppice pits), Doreen and Howard Hart (Kath's brother).

Camp Capers

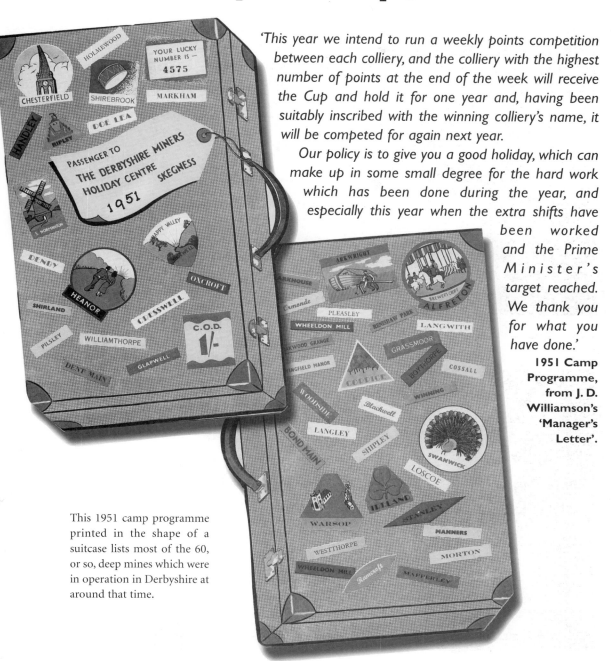

'This year we intend to run a weekly points competition between each colliery, and the colliery with the highest number of points at the end of the week will receive the Cup and hold it for one year and, having been suitably inscribed with the winning colliery's name, it will be competed for again next year.

Our policy is to give you a good holiday, which can make up in some small degree for the hard work which has been done during the year, and especially this year when the extra shifts have been worked and the Prime Minister's target reached. We thank you for what you have done.'

1951 Camp Programme, from J. D. Williamson's 'Manager's Letter'.

This 1951 camp programme printed in the shape of a suitcase lists most of the 60, or so, deep mines which were in operation in Derbyshire at around that time.

'Sunday 1.45pm

The sea is near to swim in, the sand to snooze or romp on, or – if you'd care to explore the Lincolnshire countryside in a comfortable coach, book your seat early and take a tour.'

1953 Entertainment Programme.

PROGRAMME FOR YOUR ENTERTAINMENT

Sunday

1.45 p.m. The sea is near to swim in, the sand to snooze or romp on, or— if you'd care to explore the Lincolnshire country-side in a comfortable coach, book your seat early and take a tour.

7.30 p.m. **SUMMER STARTIME**
Show business at its best, music, laughter and song — a feast of fun for everyone.

THE DERBYSHIRE MINER'S HOLIDAY CENTRE

PROGRAMME FOR YOUR ENTERTAINMENT

Monday

We search for
THE IDEAL HOLIDAY GIRL
A morning's fun for all as young ladies are interviewed for the honour of being Ideal Holiday Girl. This week's finalist will be a special guest at the "GRAND SEPTEMBER FINALS" and may win the coveted title of "IDEAL HOLIDAY GIRL 1953" together with the Special Silver Trophies and Compact.

2.15 p.m. RAINBOW RANCHERS
Repeat the promise—introduce new members.

2.30 p.m. ADULT **NOVELTY** SPORTS
A number of sporting events planned for the amusement of competitors and spectators.

6.30 p.m. "TIP - TOP - TALENT"
Children's talent competition—all ages from toddlers to fifteeners.

8.30 p.m. (or at close of talent competition).
BALLROOM REVELS
Our resident band invite you to "Take your partners."
GOOD-NIGHT
YOUR SERENADE.

THE DERBYSHIRE MINER'S HOLIDAY CENTRE

'Wednesday 9.30pm
Crinoline Capers

Most of the dances will be old time, let's see the Beau bow when requesting a dance, and the Belles curtsey in reply.'

1953 Entertainment Programme.

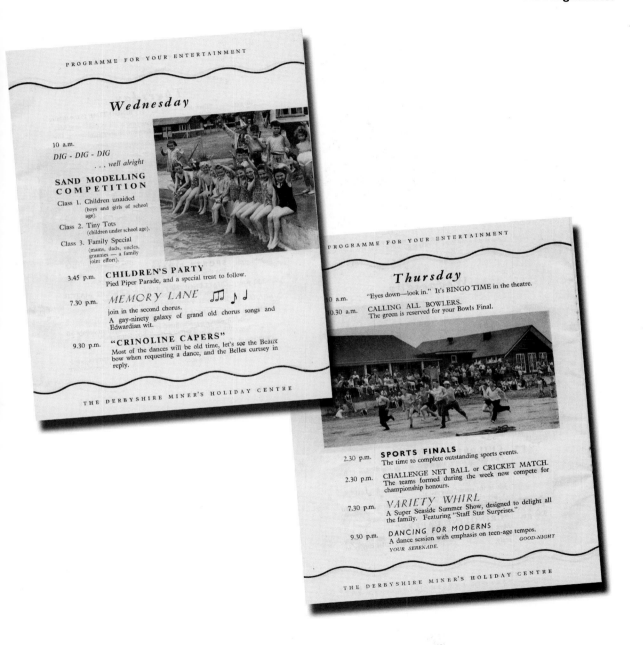

PROGRAMME FOR YOUR ENTERTAINMENT

Wednesday

10 a.m.
DIG - DIG - DIG
. . . well alright

SAND MODELLING COMPETITION

Class 1. Children unaided (boys and girls of school age).

Class 2. Tiny Tots (children under school age).

Class 3. Family Special (mams, dads, uncles, grannies — a family joint effort).

3.45 p.m. **CHILDREN'S PARTY**
Pied Piper Parade, and a special treat to follow.

7.30 p.m. *MEMORY LANE* ♫ ♪ ♩
join in the second chorus.
A gay-ninety galaxy of grand old chorus songs and Edwardian wit.

9.30 p.m. **"CRINOLINE CAPERS"**
Most of the dances will be old time, let's see the Beaux bow when requesting a dance, and the Belles curtsey in reply.

THE DERBYSHIRE MINER'S HOLIDAY CENTRE

PROGRAMME FOR YOUR ENTERTAINMENT

Thursday

10 a.m. "Eyes down—look in." It's BINGO TIME in the theatre.

10.30 a.m. **CALLING ALL BOWLERS.**
The green is reserved for your Bowls Final.

2.30 p.m. **SPORTS FINALS**
The time to complete outstanding sports events.

2.30 p.m. **CHALLENGE NET BALL or CRICKET MATCH.**
The teams formed during the week now compete for championship honours.

7.30 p.m. *VARIETY WHIRL*
A Super Seaside Summer Show, designed to delight all the family. Featuring "Staff Star Surprises."

9.30 p.m. **DANCING FOR MODERNS**
A dance session with emphasis on teen-age tempos.
YOUR SERENADE.   *GOOD-NIGHT*

THE DERBYSHIRE MINER'S HOLIDAY CENTRE

'I entered the camp's biggest biceps competition. We all had to have our biceps measured by this young woman – I can't remember her name but I know she was French. I was only 15 or 16 and I was up against the World Champion Six Inch Nail Breaking Champion himself, Mr Harold Cope of Ripley!'

Malcolm Bond, son of Ferdin Bond.

The beautiful young French assistant, complete with tape measure, about to prove who has the biggest biceps. The three main contestants seen here are, from the left: Malcolm Bond, Charlie Hollis of Ripley and the world six inch nail breaking champion Mr Harold Cope, who was a Deputy at Ripley pit.

Harold Cope, world champion strong man, can be seen breaking in half an iron bar 18 inches long and half an inch thick. Harold could break a six inch nail with his bare hands in 5.2 seconds and 5 six inch nails in 58 seconds and both of these world records still stand. The nails Harold used were specially toughened and this foiled many of the rival strong men who challenged him and failed.

One of Harold's 'heavy duty' six inch nails, given to me by his daughter Mary, is shown here, actual size.

'You'd sometimes get into a few scrapes with the rivalry between pits but it was good natured stuff really. Mind you one year I remember a bit of trouble after a football match between men from Parkhouse Pit and staff from the camp. The referee was a fella called Frank Yexley – he was a camp entertainer – and he was taking bets on the match. Well, we Parkhouse lads were good and we knew we were going to win so we slipped him our money on the side. So off we went, scoring goals of course, but he was disallowing them. Well, he nearly ended up in the sea!'

George Holmes of Clay Cross; George worked as a young man at Parkhouse Pit before setting up the bus and travel company he runs to this day.

At the camp in 1952 are the Parkhouse pit footballers, many of whom would have played in the fateful match described by George Holmes. Standing, from the left, are: Jim Sutton, George Spencer, Colin Holmes, George Holmes, George Bradley, Dennis Fellows, Dennis Lawrence, Ken Holmes, Dennis Lunn and George Finley. Kneeling, from the left, are: Geoff Wainwright, Dickie Sutton, George Muldoon, Stan Kirk, Keith Petit and Glyn Griffiths.

The villain of George's tale – publican, boxing promoter and all-round entrepreneur Frank Yexley, seen here examining feet in an impromptu 'beautiful ankles' competition.

'Marge Wardale, two doors up from us, was a good runner. She used to enter races at different competitions and she usually ended up winning. We were all young mothers at the time and we moved on to the new council estate together. I remember when they were still building some of the houses across the road we used to time Marge across the fields and my, could she shift!'

Doris Gration of Ripley.

This race took place at the camp in, I think 1950, and it shows Marge Wardale of Ripley in her usual winning position. To Marge's left is Kitty Franklin, now Kitty Jepson, of Alfreton who made these photographs available.

Frank Yexley, local Lincolnshire publican who at this time was also the sports and entertainments organiser at the camp. At the extreme right of this picture is Mrs Jepson who remembers this as an impromptu 'beautiful ankles' contest.

'My dad was a good singer and I remember one year he was up on stage and he won the Adult Talent Competition. I think he won £50. Whatever it was it seemed like a fortune at the time, more than a week's wages and more than enough to keep him going for the rest of the week at camp.'

Steve Barnet of Swanwick, father William Eric Barnet, Holmewood pit.

The Adult Talent Competition which Steve Barnet's father, Eric Barnet, won receiving a handsome cash prize. I understand that Steve's father had a particularly good voice and would often sing in the pubs and clubs. Steve seems to have inherited that musical talent and today he is an accomplished musician playing in local bands.

Eric Barnet appears on stage again, this time taking part in an unusual 'try and make me laugh if you can' competition! Judging by Eric's sombre expression he appears to be winning despite the best efforts of the man with his jacket over his head.

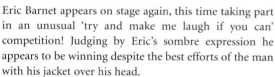

'In the early days, after the war, the union men from each pit organised a lot of the games and sport at the camp. Usually families from two or three local pits were staying at the camp at the same time so there was a lot of friendly rivalry. Football matches and tug of war were usually pit against pit.'

Fred Grace of Waingroves who worked in the pits in the Ripley area for many years, and as a pit Deputy. Fred is also a methodist lay preacher and was a local councillor and former Mayor of Ripley.

Men from Denby pit take on their rivals from Alfreton in 1952. Second from left is Fred Grace, and fifth and sixth from the left is Jack Wheatley and my father Norman Gration.

Look closely at the anchor of this team and you can see that the men from Blackwell pit have enlisted support from unusual quarters! This photograph from the mid-1950s was loaned to me by Derek Pell who is further up the rope, just out of shot of this close up.

'The competitions between each pit weren't just for the men. I remember taking part in football matches at the camp playing for the Ormonde pit Ladies team.'

Sally Burns of Heanor, her husband Harry Burns worked at Ormonde pit.

The Ormonde Ladies football team from the 1950s with Sally Burns in the back row, third from the right. Also identified in the picture are Ethel Pooler, Mrs Dawes, Mrs Marriot, Mrs Ratcliffe and Ron Dawes, son of Fred Dawes who was NUM Secretary at Ormonde at the time.

In the Ormonde Ladies tug of war of 1951 is Kath Hart, now Slaney, third from the left. To her right is her sister-in-law Doreen Hart and her sister Barbara Hart, now Needham. Urging the team on, at the right of the picture, is Kath's father Harry Hart who worked at Ormonde and Coppice pits.

'Friday, 7.30pm is TOPSY-TURVY TIME – when you change your personality and become a Pirate, Hula-Hula Girl, Cowboy, Toreador – or anything your sense of humour or imagination may suggest. Enjoy the cabaret and DANCE, SING and LAUGH until we join hands and voice in AULD LANG SYNE.'

Camp Entertainment Programme.

Topsy-Turvy Night from the mid-1950s with four campers enacting a mock wedding. The 'preacher' to the left is Jim Longmate who worked regular 'nights' at Moreton pit. The 'groom' is Jim Stone, also of Moreton pit.

Later in the 1970s and perhaps reflecting the more relaxed attitude of the times, Topsy-Turvy Night became exclusively when 'Ladies dress as Men – Men dress as ladies!' Opposite are two Friday Topsy-Turvy revellers from the 1970s.

'I remember fancy dress competitions, sand castle building competitions, knobbly knees, talent shows and men's egg and spoon races. Everybody joined in then, didn't they? As Mum used to say, there was very little money, so people were used to making their own entertainment. Going to the 'theatre' was an occasion then, and to buy a bag of sweets to eat while you watched the entertainment was really living!'

Janet Wright.

Men from pits in the Ripley and Alfreton area have a go at the egg and spoon race. In the background, looking on, are Jack Wheatley and Norman Gration from Ripley.

Men from the same pits line up for the sack race. Second from the right is Les Bridges from Ripley and fourth from the right is, I believe, Geoff Gale also from Ripley. Fred Grace from Waingroves is standing at the back fifth from the left.

'LEND A HAND ON THE SAND.

Bring your bucket, bring your spade,
And hurry to the sand.
There are castles to be made,
So lend a helping hand.
Come Mum, come Dad, come cousin Joe,
Come all shapes and sizes,
Come on Granny – Have a go!
There are lots of lovely prizes.'

Camp Entertainment Programme, 10.00am, Wednesdays.

Nick Bernard and Mick Millington 'doing the rounds' judging the various sand castle entries.

The Eyley family and friends of Blackwell pose in front of their 'Miners' Welfare' built as their entry in the sand castle competition. Sitting in the deck chairs, from the left, are: Albert Eyley, Rene Eyley and Phyllis Sales. On the sand, from the left, are: Jack Aldred, Brian Eyley, Dave Eyley, Melvin Aldred, Eric Eyley and Bet Aldred.

'In the early days at the camp the mining families would have a go at anything. We had all sorts of competitions and talent shows and most of them would have a go. Later on though people didn't seem so keen. I don't know whether people were just getting so used to watching television or whether it was just that there were so many good acts to watch at the camp but things were different.'

Avis Millington.

These photographs of a girls' and ladies' skipping competition were loaned to me by Kathleen Marsden of Alfreton, whose father was miner Earnest Bearder. These competitions are examples of the more informal and community based activities which were typical of life at the camp in the 1940s and early 1950s.

'Ladies taking a break at the Miners' Holiday Camp at Skegness were invited to sew a patch on the seat of a man's pants — and the fastest was the winner. It was obviously a contest which had them in stitches, and woe betide anyone who got a little behind in their work!'

Alfreton and Ripley Echo.

Winifred Bennett of Alfreton gets to work sewing a patch on to Sib Dennis, a family friend. Winifred, who was the eventual winner of this competition, remembers receiving a commemorative scroll which she kept for many years. Winifred's daughter, Kath Cook, was the youngest of eight children and she remembers going to the camp every year. Her father Sydney Bennett worked at Alfreton pit.

This mother and baby competition shows at the right of the group Mrs Edna Grace of Waingroves, wife of Fred Grace, with their youngest son, Roger. In the middle of the group is, I believe, my Aunt Bertha with her daughter Christine, and my mother and me. Unfortunately, I am not able to identify the rather large baby with the ribbon and bottle, third from the right.

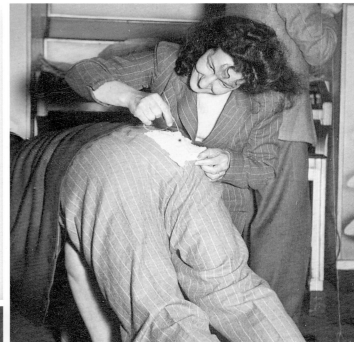

'Donkey Derby day was great fun. The man who hired out donkeys on the beach used to bring them up into the camp one day each week. Most of the campers would have a go, husbands, wives and children of course! Sometimes people would bet on who was going to win.'

Avis Millington.

On the donkey at the far right is Mr Eyre from Danesmoor, Chesterfield.

Len Madely of Loscoe can just be seen behind the front donkey offering encouragement to the rider, his daughter Sylvia Madely. Len worked at Ormonde pit.

'It was always fun and games at the camp. People used to just get stuck in. I remember Benny Barker, a family friend and miner from Blackwell, riding in the donkey derby at the camp.'

Kathryn Bennett, now Kath Cook, whose father Sydney worked at Alfreton pit.

Men from the Alfreton and Swanwick pits ride it out in this donkey derby. Benny (William) Barker from Blackwell can be seen giving it some 'yeehaa!' on the donkey second from the right.

The 'donkey man' getting to grips with these young riders in a photograph from Mrs Marsden of Oakerthorpe near Alfreton.

'10.00am THURSDAY
TREASURE HUNT

Mums and Dads will hunt for treasure by following the rhyming clues.
Kiddies, follow Jolly Jack in search of surprises.'

Camp Entertainment Programme.

This photograph, loaned by Ray Madely, shows what we believe is part of the camp's weekly treasure hunt. Unfortunately, I am not able to identify anyone in this photograph other than Frank Yexley, the camp's first entertainment supervisor, who can be seen at the left above.

In this wheelbarrow race Margaret Bennett from Alfreton is on the ground laughing, having been abandoned by her race partner Albert Riley. In the background, to the right, the rest of the Bennett family look on.

'I remember every year Terry Thompson, an Alfreton miner, used to win the sack bag race. He used to shout: "No man in a sack bag is going to beat me!"'

Kathryn Bennett, now Kath Cook, whose father Sydney worked at the Alfreton pit.

First from the left, Terry Thompson from Alfreton gets off to a flying start in the sack race. As usual Terry won this race.

Families from the Alfreton and Swanwick pits line up for the wheelbarrow race. Fourth from the left with her dress tucked into her knickers is Margaret Bennett. Third from the left is Margaret's race partner, Alfreton miner, Albert Riley.

'In my day I wasn't a bad runner, so I used to enter most of the races when I was at the miners' camp. One year – 1951 I think it was – I remember we had to have a re-run of the 200 yards race. The chap who won the first time cheated, but the second time round I crossed the line first.'

Derek Pell of South Normanton who worked at the Blackwell pits.

Second from the right, Derek Pell lines up for the second time for the start of this re-run of the 200-yard race.

Below, Derek approaches the finishing line to win this race.

The photograph below shows the first attempt at this race with Derek in second position. But, as Derek explains above, the winner of this first race cheated and a re-run was called for.

'We went every year to the miners' camp — uncles, aunts, the whole lot of us. You just went automatically — every year you put your name down for a chalet. But the men never changed into holiday clothes. They always wore their navy blue suits — even though it meant rolling up their trouser legs for the knobbly knees contest!'

Kathleen Marsden, her father, Earnest Bearder, worked all his life at Alfreton pit.

Miners from the Alfreton and Swanwick area on parade before the knobbly knees competition. Earnest Bearder of Alfreton worked all his life underground, from the age of 13 until he retired just before Alfreton pit was closed. He can be seen at the end of the parade above and in the photograph extreme right.

Mick Millington looks on as the regulation 'long Johns' are adjusted in this Knobbly Knees competition. The little girl in the background is Susan Clarke of Ripley.

'Winner of the darts championship finals for the William Younger Cup was Mr R. Laws representing Harworth Colliery who beat Mr B. Tomlinson of Hardy Lane Chesterfield. The MC was Doug Sorby'.

The *Derbyshire Times*, 21 September 1962.

Unfortunately, I don't have a photograph of Mr Laws being presented with the William Younger Cup as reported in the *Derbyshire Times*. However, the photograph above shows another recipient of the cup, Ron Greaves, after this darts tournament in the Tavern bar in 1949. Standing, from the left, are: Roy Longmate and George Bower. Seated, from the left, are: Sel Greaves, Len Greaves, Ron Greaves and Sel Blount. I believe all the men worked at Shirland pit.

The children of Mr and Mrs Jack Davies with their 'cups' after winning in the children's races. Jack Davies worked at Alfreton pit for 22 years before it closed in 1968.

'We went to the camp for years, from when the kids were little to when they were grown up. One of the last times I went I was a grandmother and so I ended up in the Glamorous Grandmother competition!'

Joyce Morris, of Poolsbrook near Chesterfield

The Glamorous Grandmother competition was one of the enduring features of camp life, as this compilation spanning nearly 40 years shows. From the 1980s, is glamorous grandmother Joyce Morris of Poolsbrook (left).

Mrs M. Eyre (right) of Danesmoor, Chesterfield, on stage in 1949 with Frank Yexley. This photograph was given many years ago to Avis Millington by Mrs Eyre. Though I'm not entirely sure that it shows the Glamorous Grandmother competition, Mrs Eyre has written on the back of the photograph 'When entertainment was in the open owing to the lack of a proper building'.

Glamorous grandmother Mrs Fanny Robinson (above), on stage in the 1940s with Frank Yexley the camp's first entertainment organiser. Mrs Robinson's husband, John William Robinson, worked at Markham pit until he was forced to retire through ill health.

'I remember the little train they had at the miners' camp. It was a proper steam train on a circular track and you could sit on the back of it. It was great fun but unfortunately I haven't got a photograph of it. I'd love to see it again.'

Kevin Neale, of Mastin Moor near Chesterfield.

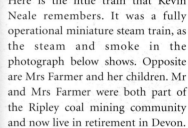

Here is the little train that Kevin Neale remembers. It was a fully operational miniature steam train, as the steam and smoke in the photograph below shows. Opposite are Mrs Farmer and her children. Mr and Mrs Farmer were both part of the Ripley coal mining community and now live in retirement in Devon.

'I remember the whole family being on stage taking part in the Happy Families Competition. The idea was you had to answer questions on why you thought you were the happiest family at the camp. I remember thinking that we're going to win this, until my husband Harry said: "We're happy because I'm the boss!"'

Sally Burns, of Heanor, whose husband Harry worked at Ripley and Ormonde pits.

Mr and Mrs Burns with their children Brenda, John and Christine on stage in the 1950s with Nick Bernard taking part in the Happy Families competition.

Another family competition from the 1950s, with Mick Millington.

'When I was an Ideal Holiday Girl in 1960 I felt as though I had to be on my best behaviour, though normally I'd let my hair down a bit. We used to get up to some daft things, but nothing by today's standards. There's this photograph of me and some of my friends taking off the Tiller Girls walking through the camp.'

Sandra Turner of Arkwright, whose father Roland 'Toby' Turner worked at Arkwright pit.

Sandra Turner and her friends as the Tiller Girls at the camp in 1961. From the left are: Mary Longdon, Hazel Hopkinson, Sandra Turner and Nilla Cropper. I love those 1960s slacks and mohair sweaters!

It seems that Sandra wasn't the only member of the Turner family able to let their hair down a bit. Getting a lift back to camp is Sandra's mother, Gertrude, riding on Sandra's father, Roland 'Toby' Turner.

'BALLOON CONTEST
£15 for One Shilling

Launch your gas-filled balloon on the wings of the wind. The further it goes, the better your chance. Last year's winner – Sheila Anthony, 11 Barkham Crescent, Fern Road, Low Gates, Staveley. Her balloon was returned from ZEELAND, HOLLAND.'

Camp Programme, 1951.

YOU COULD WIN
£100
IN OUR 1957 BALLOON RACE

HERE'S A REALLY HAPPY FAMILY!

GEOFFREY GALE, 11 Ash Crescent, Ripley, (representing Denby Hall Colliery) proudly displays the cheque for ONE HUNDRED POUNDS he received as the winner of our 1956 Balloon Race.

FOR FULL DETAILS SEE DOUGIE
£100 MAY BE WAITING FOR YOU!

26

The Ideal Holiday Girls

' 'Big Jack' Simpson used to get the girls from the audience up on stage for the Ideal Holiday Girl Competitions. We'd say to Jack "She looks a likely candidate down there", and he'd go down and often end up picking them up in his arms and carrying them onto the stage.'

Harvey Mellors, camp photographer.

One Ideal Holiday Girl from 1957 who remembers being carried on stage in this way is Margaret Boulton, now Mansell, shown here.

'Big Jack' Simpson deposits on stage a likely Ideal Holiday Girl contestant he has just 'lifted' from the theatre audience! Harvey Mellors assures me that Big Jack's technique was guaranteed to get the competition going with a swing.

'I remember the Ideal Holiday Girl competition and being picked up out of my seat by this big chap and being carried to the stage. I must have mentioned to Mick Millington that I'd been dancing the night before with Maurice Stanley because they soon had him up on stage as well.'

Margaret Boulton, now Mansell, who was an Ideal Holiday Girl in 1957.

One of the weekly Ideal Holiday Girl competitions from 1957 with Margaret Boulton on stage with her dancing partner Maurice Stanley. The compères are, to the left Nick Bernard, and to the right Mick Millington. Margaret tells me that in this picture Nick was busy quizzing her and Maurice about the previous night's dance.

Margaret was the eventual winner of that week's Ideal Holiday Girl competition, and here she is with her fellow contestants.

'We used to go to the camp in the 1940s and 1950s and more than once I ended up on stage with the likes of Mick Millington for the Ideal Holiday Girl competition. Years later in Benidorm – I think it was 1986 – this man came up to me and said "Hello Miss Bennett, what are you doing here?" It was Mick Millington! He hadn't changed a bit and I'll never know how he remembered me after all those years.'

Margaret Bennett, now Margaret Scott, whose father Sydney worked at Alfreton pit.

Right: Margaret Bennett on stage in 1952, not with Mick Millington on this occasion but with Nick Bernard and, on his knees, Cyril Elliott the organist.

Margaret was the eventual winner of this particular contest and here she is third from the left with her fellow contestants. Also on stage below are Mavis Storer, Shirley Presland, Beryl Shinfield and Vanda Drew one of the camp entertainers.

'I was an Ideal Holiday Girl in 1952 and a runner-up the year before. Although you were dragged up on stage you didn't mind being there really. I knew they'd ask me embarrassing questions like "do you have a boyfriend" so I decided beforehand to say "no"!'

Margaret Bennett, now Margaret Scott, whose father Sydney worked at Alfreton pit.

Margaret Bennett at left of picture as runner up of the Ideal Holiday Girl contest for Alfreton and Swanwick pits' week in 1951. Margaret remembers that the girl wearing the Ideal Holiday Girl sash in this picture was also called Margaret and that she came from Swanwick.

A group of very happy holidaymakers at the camp in 1949 gathered around the Ideal Holiday Girl winner for that particular week. This photograph was given to Avis Millington by Mrs Eyre of Chesterfield.

'I was Miss Arkwright in the end of season finals in 1960. In that year Arkwright, Ireland, Renishaw Park and Wilsthorpe pits were at the camp in the last week of the season so I stayed on over the weekend with my Dad for the finals.'

Sandra Turner of Arkwright.

Sandra Turner wearing her 'Miss Arkwright' sash in the 1960 end of season Ideal Holiday Girl finals. The winner of each week's title throughout the season was invited to attend the finals. Later the title was changed to the annual Coal Queen of Britain and the competition was broadened to include the wives and daughters of miners from across the country.

Sandra wears the Ideal Holiday Girl sash and poses with the other contestants for the week in 1960 when the Arkwright, Ireland, Renishaw Park and Wilsthorpe pits were staying at the camp.

'To be honest, being ideal Holiday Girl took the gloss off my week at the camp. There was a lot of pressure on you as Ideal Holiday Girl. You had to take part in all those photo sessions and judge children's competitions and things like that. You felt you couldn't relax and let your hair down because you were expected to set a good example.'

Sandra Turner of Arkwright.

Sandra Turner wearing her 1960 Ideal Holiday Girl sash with her father Roland 'Toby' Turner who worked at Arkwright pit. Although Sandra tells us of the down side of being an Ideal Holiday Girl, there's no mistaking in this photograph the pride of both father and daughter.

It was Mary Longdon who was Arkwright's winner of this 1961 Ideal Holiday Girl competition. Sandra Turner can be seen to the left of Mary. Also in the picture are Mick Millington, Mike Dennett and another blue coat called Patti.

'I was an Ideal Holiday Girl in both 1958 and 1959. I remember the first time saying that my favourite hobby was swimming and having to lie across a chair on stage doing the breaststroke. Well, they got a hose pipe and said not to worry, there was no water, and the next thing I knew I was being drenched!'

**Janet Eyley, now Janet Coope, of Blackwell
whose father Albert Eyley worked at Blackwell pit until it closed in 1970.**

Top left: Janet Eyley representing Blackwell pit in the end of season Ideal Holiday Girl finals.

Top right: Janet in 1959 officiating at a children's fancy dress competition in her capacity as Ideal Holiday Girl for that particular week.

Bottom: Although Janet won the Ideal Holiday Girl title in both her weeks in 1958 and 1959, in this picture she poses with the other contestants and the winner from, I believe, 1960.

'MONDAY 10.00AM – THIS WEEK'S IDEAL HOLIDAY GIRL

A competition for girls of over school leaving age. This week's finalist is invited to enter for the close of season IDEAL HOLIDAY GIRL 1951 contest and will be an honoured guest for the final weekend CLOSE OF SEASON CELEBRATIONS. Girls of school age are invited to enter for the JUNIOR MISS competition.'

Camp Entertainment Programme.

This photograph of the close of season Ideal Holiday Girl finals is from the early 1950s. Mick Millington and General Manager J. D. Williamson are to the right of the picture. Note the relative simplicity of the presentation of this early competition compared to the final just a few years later in 1957.

Winnie Holmes, now Wilkinson, was the Ideal Holiday Girl for the Heanor pits' week in 1953.

The winner of the 1957 finals, Ann Hawkins of Heage representing Ripley pit, was described by the *Derbyshire Times* as a '16-year-old blonde' and a fine athlete, 'having won the Derbyshire County 150 yards Championship in record time.'

'FINALS WEEKEND AT SKEGNESS CENTRE

The main event was on Sunday when awards were presented following the selection of the Ideal Holiday Girl. The compères, Mick Millington and Nick Bernard, asked each contestant the same three questions. What is the most urgent need of teenagers today? What makes you laugh? If you could have one wish granted, what would it be? One reply to the first question was: "My Dad says a good hiding, but he's no judge!" The girls were judged for appearance, personality, poise and decorum with the winner receiving the Waleswood Trophy.'

The *Derbyshire Times*, 23 September 1960.

I am unable to name Miss Shirebrook, though I do know this is an earlier contest, probably around 1958.

Here is a selection of finalists from the late 1950s and early 1960s. Above, I'm not able to name Miss Whitwell, though I believe this picture may be from 1961 or 1963. Opposite is the 1959 winner Iris Yates, described by the *Derbyshire Times* as 'a 17-year-old student of music and geography from Arkwright near Chesterfield'. The young girl at the left of this picture is Mick Millington's daughter Georgina who was usually called upon to help present the prizes.

'DERBYSHIRE MINERS FINALS WEEKEND AT SKEGNESS

It was Finals Weekend at the Derbyshire Miners' Welfare Holiday Centre at Skegness where the winners of the weekly competitions met to compete for the various awards. The winner of the Ideal Holiday Girl finals was Hazel Hoskin, aged 16, who lives at 27 Danby Avenue, Old Whittington, Chesterfield and who was representing Bolsover Colliery. She won the Waleswood Trophy and the Derbyshire Times silver compact, £25 to spend on clothes and a week's free holiday at the Centre.'
Derbyshire Times, 21 September 1962.

Sixteen-year-old Hazel Hoskin receives the Waleswood Trophy as the 1962 Ideal holiday Girl. Accompanying Mick Millington on this occasion is Patti, one of the camp's bluecoats. The *Derbyshire Times* report on these end of season finals also records that one of the main founders of the camp, Harry Hicken, was present. The report notes: 'Mr H. Hicken, now aged 80 and described by Mr Wynn as the architect of the idea for the Centre, recalled that when the Centre was opened in 1939 miners and their families had a first-class holiday there for about 30 shillings each. There was then a staff of 80 and now it had risen to 320.'

The 16 competitors for the 1962 end of season Ideal Holiday Girl finals. Hazel Hoskin, the eventual winner, can be seen in the second row, second from the right. Third from the right, standing next to Hazel, is Marilyn Wardale of Ripley representing Swanwick pit. Marilyn and I went to the same school and she lived two doors up from me. The other finalists in this picture are: Janet Bailey (Warsop Main), Barbara Wilson (Langwith), Patricia Place (Welbeck), Gwen Harrison (Ripley), Mary Watt (Derby), Vivien Vaughan (Cadeby), Jean Hallowes (Westhorpe), Jean Sherman (Oxcroft), Sharron Marriott (Shipley Coppice), Glenys Bowman (Nottingham), Norma Crockett (A Winning), Margaret Kinton (Cossall), Stella Argyle (Ashton-on-Trent), Christine Moss (Holmewood).

'FINALS WEEKEND AT DERBYSHIRE MINERS' HOLIDAY CENTRE

This has been the most successful season ever — and there have been 17 of them — at the Derbyshire Miners' Holiday Centre at Skegness. The best weather for many years played a large part in this. During Grand Finals Weekend, Mr H. W. Wynn, General Secretary to the Derbyshire Area NUM, told a packed Centre that over the season 22,000 people had been accommodated, 2,500 more than last year and there had been hundreds more day visitors. There were 14 finalists on Sunday for the Ideal Holiday Girl title, and the winner was 19-year-old Angela Ridgers, of 12 Walnut Close Chellaston, Derby, a copy typist.'

Derbyshire Times, 18 September 1964.

The 1964 final winner, Angela Ridgers. The *Derbyshire Times* report of these finals notes: 'The verdict was a close one, the other most attractive finalists being Natalia Bratsch (Ormonde), Sylvia James (Blackwell), Gail Brammer (Derby), Joan Dunn (Creswell), Gillian Spencer (Eastwood), Joan Pinchin (Whitwell), Joyce Cartledge (Langwith), Valerie Pollard (Shepshed), Janet Griffiths (Chesterfield), Julia Batty (Eckington), Jacky Eaton (Ripley), Shirley Bolland and Alice Mullen (Bullcroft).

The winner of the 1964 finals, Angela Ridgers, is flanked by the other finalists and various 'dignitaries' who included Bert Wynn, NUM, Councillor and Mrs A. Wise and Herbert Parkin, NUM Compensation Agent who I always knew as 'the Compen Man'.

'LOCAL WINNERS AT SKEGNESS HOLIDAY CENTRE FINALS

Competitors from all over the country flocked to the Derbyshire Miners' Holiday Centre at the weekend for the Gala Finals of competitions which have been held at the camp every week during the season. Among the winners were three local competitors while the others came from as far away as London in the south and Durham in the north. The 'Search for the Stars' talent competition attracted many entries during the season and a Shirebrook man, Mr Patrick Scholes of 12, The Coppice, came out on top. The beauty competitions were both won by local girls. The title of Bathing Beauty went to 20-year-old Karen Fields of 34 William Avenue, Eastwood. The Ideal Holiday Girl competition was won by 21-year-old Theresa Burdett of 11 Nethercroft Lane, Danesmoor.'

The *Derbyshire Times*, 27 September 1968.

Left: As reported by the *Derbyshire Times*, the three 'local winners' in the 1968 end of season finals. Left to right: Theresa Burdett, Ideal Holiday Girl, Patrick Scholes, talent competition winner, Karen Fields, Bathing Beauty.

Right: Theresa Burdett takes centre-stage with the winning Waleswood Trophy, her cheque for £15 and her *Derbyshire Times* vanity case.

'COAL QUEEN OF BRITAIN CONTEST 1970

Lovely girls from all the coalfields will soon be bidding for a chance to win the 1970 Coal Queen of Britain crown. And for those who get through to the glittering final in Skegness, there is a weekend of breath-taking excitement, says last year's winner, Rose McLachlan. "It was a fabulous, thrilling experience," she added, "and judging by the even bigger prize list, this year's final should be the greatest. I only wish I could have another go at it!"

All over Britain union teams and mining folk are busily arranging their local Coal Queen dances and events to find the 15 finalists who will travel like queens by train to Skegness — all arranged by British Rail.'

Camp Entertainment Programme.

Rose McLachlan wearing the Coal Queen crown, with Mick Millington in 1969. This was the first year the title was introduced and it drew contestants from all British coalfields, reflecting the declining numbers of Derbyshire mining families and the camp's growing trend to attract visitors from further afield. Although the Ideal Holiday Girl title continued for some years, it was somewhat overshadowed by the high profile marketing and sponsorship of the Coal Queen title. At the time, the prize for the Ideal Holiday Girl winner was £15 or £20, compared to the 1970 Coal Queen top prize of £1,200!

Who will be Coal Queen of Britain 1970?

COAL NEWS

Come and see — and enjoy this great family weekend of fun

Coal Queen of Britain Final, Skegness, Sept. 26, 1970
Book now for this weekend of a lifetime ... the Coal Queen parade, concert and ball, with comfortable accommodation, fine catering — and all the fun of the Skegness Miners' Holiday Centre.
From lunch-time on Saturday, September 26 to after lunch on Sunday, September 27, all-in cost is £2 15s. for each adult; £2 for each child from six to fifteen; and £1 5s. for each child under six.
Fill up the coupon now, and send to : Manager, Derbyshire Miners' Holiday Centre, Coal Queen of Britain Contest, Skegness, Lincs.

Rose McLachlan again in this advertisement for the 1970 Coal Queen competition from the National Coal Board's newspaper, *Coal News*.

Mick Millington

'Kiddies make sure you meet Uncle Mick at your own centre designed exclusively for you THE MINER'S MINOR'

Camp entertainment programme, 1954.

EXTRA SPECIAL!
YOUR KIDDIES WILL ENJOY THEMSELVES WITH UNCLE MICK MILLINGTON

The Jolly Goblin Dancing Girls

Here's the winner

... and a young artiste

We have pleasure in announcing
THE CHILDREN'S NEW RENDEZVOUS

The JOLLY GOBLIN THEATRE

YET ANOTHER ADDED ATTRACTION FOR 1954

AMUSEMENTS
SPORTS — GAMES
DANCING — TEA PARTY
FILM SHOWS
VARIETY SHOWS
TALENT — COMPETITIONS — OUTINGS
PRIZES

Kiddies - make sure you meet "Uncle Mick"
AT YOUR OWN CENTRE DESIGNED EXCLUSIVELY FOR YOU
THE MINER'S MINOR

As these extracts from camp entertainment programmes make clear (above 1963, opposite 1954) Mick Millington was a clear favourite with the 'miner's minor'! The Jolly Goblin Theatre referred to opposite was created from the old children's dormitory on the sea front when the new brick dormitory was built.

Mick E Millington – Entertainment Supervisor

Once again to meet and greet you is our cheery Entertainment Supervisor, 'Uncle Mick' to every child and just 'Mick' to the adults, his lean figure, large feet and smiling eyes an asset to camp activities. He is the official trouble eraser, brow smoother, baby calmer, beer taster – and Friend to all – on stage, or sports arena. Signature tune: 'When you're smiling'. Ambition: To keep you gay by night and day.

Nick Bernard – Comedian and Stage Supervisor

In addition to his familiar role as resident 'Shriek of Mirth', Nick will also be responsible for the supervision of all stage productions. Nick has had varied entertainment experience in many parts of the world – straight actor, comedian, radio compere and B.B.C script writer. Signature tune: 'Ma! He's making eyes at me'. Ambition: To cheer old friends and make new friends.

Hal 'Nobby' Marta

Your 'melody man' needs little introduction, possessing a fine resonant voice and an engaging cheerful personality. 'Nobby' has proved himself a firm favourite with young and old. This season he has extended his repertoire and will again delight all with his rendition of favourite songs. Signature tune: 'Without a song'. Ambition: To remain your melody man.

'Mick, Nick and Nobby! Three great chaps – they made the place. Mick hadn't got airs and graces about him, you just liked him and he made you feel at home.'
Kathleen Hart, now Slaney, of Ilkeston

The attributes of Mick, Nick and Nobby are summarised is this extract from an early camp entertainment programme

Kathleen Hart in the centre of this picture with Mick and Nobby, and to the left is her sister Barbara Hart, now Needham. To the right is Barbara Baldwin.

'MINERS' HOLIDAY CENTRE SKEGNESS, PERSONALITY PARADE NO. 1 – MICK MILLINGTON

Probably the best known of the entertainment staff at the Derbyshire Miners' Holiday Centre at Skegness is 'Uncle' Mick Millington, more affectionately known as 'Big feet'. Mick is in charge of children's entertainment at the Centre, a department for which he is particularly suited as he has a great understanding of the younger generation, and during his many years at the camp he has made thousands of friends among Derbyshire miners and their families. Mick is also an accomplished musician, has a fine singing voice and is a good comedian.'

Derbyshire Times.

Left: With his irrepressible personality, Mick could be found larking about anywhere in the camp. In this impromptu shot Mick invites the campers to follow him for a drink in the 'Follow Me Inn' in the theatre complex refurbished in 1957.

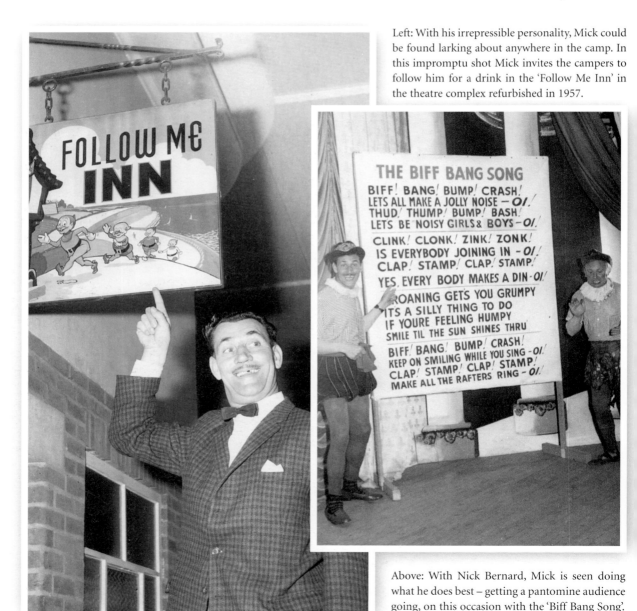

Above: With Nick Bernard, Mick is seen doing what he does best – getting a pantomine audience going, on this occasion with the 'Biff Bang Song'.

'*After the war Mick was singing in the pubs and working men's clubs around Mablethorpe and Skegness. Frank Yexley was organising the entertainment at the camp at that time and he suggested Mick should come over and help him out. In the early days Mick would lend a hand to anything and helped with maintenance out of season. Eventually, he became Entertainment Manager and out of season he would tour around Derbyshire entertaining mining families at the Miners' Welfare clubs.*'

Avis Millington.

In the early 1950s. By now, Mick was employed at the camp full-time and he and Avis were living on site. Here Mick can be seen lending a hand with general maintenance of the camp out of season.

In the Denby Miners' Welfare in 1951. Another one of Mick's jobs out of season was to tour the Miners' Welfares of Derbyshire entertaining mining families. Mick's toothy grin is instantly recognisable at the back of the group. Third from the left is Mr Fothergill of Derby Road, Denby and Mr George Butler, also of Denby, is at the right of the picture leaning on what I think is a piano.

'Mick and Avis Millington were like 'Mr and Mrs Derbyshire Miners' Holiday Camp'. Mick was the life and soul of the place. I remember the summer of 1984 – the year of the strike – we'd had no money coming into the house for months and we bumped into Mick outside the camp. "What are you doing out here!" he said "Get in that camp and enjoy yourself! I'll get it sorted for you." And he did, Mick was that sort of chap.'

Joyce Morris of Poolsbrook near Chesterfield.

Joyce Morris on the left of the photograph with Mick Millington at the camp in the mid 1980s.

'Mr and Mrs Derbyshire Miners' Holiday Camp' themselves. This photograph was taken not long after Mick and Avis's retirement from the camp.

'Both Mick and I worked at the camp from 1949 until it closed in the early 1990s. I think we were the longest serving members of staff at the camp. In all those years we saw many changes. We saw the camp facilities grow and develop, and the entertainment become more professional with bigger acts. We made so many friends, with the campers and the staff who came and went.'

Avis Millington.

These two photographs span almost the entire history of the camp and both of them include Mick and Avis. The photograph above shows many of the camp staff, and some of their children, at the camp at Christmas 1949. Mick and Avis are at the

extreme right of the picture with the young Georgina on Avis's lap. Camp boss, J. D. Williamson is standing second from the left and his wife and daughter Pat are sitting third from the left. Walter Dawes the camp's butcher is identifiable at the back still wearing his apron, and George Worsley the chef is in his whites. The photograph opposite shows Mick and Avis with many of the camp's staff from the 1980s. The singer Rosemary Squires is standing third from the right.

'I grew up in Nottingham as a publican's daughter so I suppose it wasn't surprising that I ended up working in all of the bars at the camp, the Tavern bar, the Follow Me Inn, Johnny's bar and the El Cubana.'

Avis Millington.

This compilation shows the several bars which were developed in the 1950s and 1960s as part of a growing commercialisation of the camp's facilities. Due to the influence of one of the main founding fathers of the camp, union leader and methodist lay preacher Harry Hicken, the camp was originally designed with no licensed facilities at all. Above, Avis Millington is fifth from the left, and opposite second from the right.

'Mick was always on the entertainment side but I had a lot of different jobs, mostly working in the bars and working with the children. Our own two children – Georgina and Martin – also worked at the camp and they still work in entertainment today. Gina still appears in pantomime and Martin is the manager of a big night club in Manchester.'

Avis Millington.

Throughout her 40 years at the camp Avis lent a hand to most things, including working in the bars and helping out with looking after and entertaining the children. In the middle of this group, is Avis the 'green coat' with Mick standing behind her.

Martin Millington, standing next to his father Mick, supervises the action in the camp's amusement arcade in the 1980s.

Gina Millington on the piano, with Shirley and Wendy at the opening of the Golden Butterfly Ballroom in 1966. Gina was a talented dancer and appeared in many of the camp's stage shows and she also worked as a green coat at the camp. She lives in Blackpool now and still appears in pantomine.

'Mick Millington was the envy of every Derbyshire Miner. He was a tall, good looking fella, a bit like an old fashioned film star and a grand chap. I'd say every mining family in Derbyshire had a photograph of Mick in the house.'

George Holmes of Clay Cross.

To prove George Holmes' point, I have to say that the single most popular picture shown to me by the many families I visited were the photographs of young children on stage with Mick. Clockwise, starting from top left are: Janet Wrigley (now Janet Wright of Spinkhill), John Grace of Waingroves; Jim Franklin originally of Alfreton; and Susan Duffield (now Susan Pritchett of Langley Mill).

'I remember Mick Millington and being on stage with my cousin Margaret Sales. We took part in the children's talent competition and I remember we sang Always — I will love you always.'

Janet Eyley, now Janet Coope of Blackwell, whose father
Albert Eyley worked at Blackwell pit until it closed in 1970.

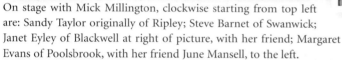

On stage with Mick Millington, clockwise starting from top left are: Sandy Taylor originally of Ripley; Steve Barnet of Swanwick; Janet Eyley of Blackwell at right of picture, with her friend; Margaret Evans of Poolsbrook, with her friend June Mansell, to the left.

'I remember being on stage with Mick Millington in the children's talent competition. I remember I recited 'The Queen of Hearts'. I didn't win! There were lots of other more talented kids than me.'

Kathryn Bennett, now Kath Cook, whose father Sydney worked at Alfreton pit.

On stage with Mick Millington, clockwise starting from the top left are: Margaret Smith originally of Alfreton with her cousin Eileen Wall; Susan Clarke originally of Ripley; Kathryn Cook of Alfreton; Kenneth Capewell originally of Loscoe.

'There were three of us up on stage singing together and because I was the smallest I was supposed to be Sandi Shaw. I knew we were in trouble when I had to explain to Mick Millington who I was supposed to be. We came third; mind you there were only three acts in the competition that night!'

Kevin Harris, originally of Alfreton, whose father Ray worked at Pyehill pit.

On stage with Mick Millington, clockwise starting from top left are: Graham Harris with Tony Birch and Kevin Harris originally of Alfreton; Lynne Glen; Carol Glen; Lenny Glen. The Glen family is from Loscoe, Heanor.

The Entertainers

'Stars such as these for your Entertainment!

Tony Melody, the star of our show.

Our Principal Comedian whose home is in Leeds, regularly appears with Harry Worth and Jimmy Clitheroe on TV and Radio. We are sure you are going to like his humour.'

Camp Entertainment Programme 1963 season.

Stars such as these for your Entertainment!

The Melotones present an unusual combination of clever dogs, with a high standard of singing ability. Both come from theatrical families.

TINO VALDI

We are very pleased to welcome Tino back again for 1963. He represented Great Britain at the International Singing Contest, and was awarded the European Cup (Coup d'Europe) and was principal singer with the Bruce Forsyth 'I'm in Charge' Show.

TONY MELODY

Our Principal Comedian whose home is in Leeds, appears regularly with Harry Worth and Jimmy Clitheroe on T.V. and Radio. We are sure you are going to like his humour.

THE MELOTONES

Eric Martin — a young singing guitarist in the Frank Ifield style, who has a popular appeal to both young and old.

We are pleased to welcome back Margaret. Her music has given a great deal of pleasure each season, she is held in highest esteem by artistes and guests alike for her brilliant accompaniment.

The Mara Sisters — Two charming young ladies who live in Lancashire, and have just returned from Beirut and India.

Duo Versatiles — Bernie and Patricia, who have a wide variety of different spots, including - Indian Fire Eating, Clowning, Balloonology, Comedy - Magic, etc.

ERIC MARTIN

MARA SISTERS

DUO VERSATILES

MARGARET CLARK

MICK MILLINGTON

Mick, who has been one of the most popular childrens entertainers for many years is this year concentrating more on entertaining the mums and dads. His very fine acting ability, pleasant voice and personality make him a very versatile entertainer.

'Everyone knew and loved the 'vivacious Vanda' – Vanda Drew. What a full figure! She made a few heads turn. As well as performing on stage, Vanda was equally at home chasing around with the kids. Then there was Pat 'Ginger' Bowman another children's entertainer. What Vanda didn't get up to, Pat would!'

Shirley Crook, now Shirley Mellors.

This compilation shows some of the many sides of the versatile and vivacious Vanda Drew. Top picture, on stage with Nick Bernard; immediately above, in the role that most children will remember Vanda, as general prankster and children's entertainer; opposite, playing her part in a knife throwing act at the camp (I think the man is Eddie of the double act Eddie and Pauline).

' 'Big Jack' Simpson was a fun character — he was a children's and theatre entertainer. Jack was to be seen during the winter months at Midlands' fairgrounds, amongst other things, 'guessing your weight', and if he failed he gave you a 'Peruvian' gold ring! He was also to be seen on the High Streets of Midlands' towns selling Old Moore's Almanacs.'

Shirley Crook, now Shirley Mellors.

Here's 'Big Jack' Simpson with his arms around Vanda Drew (left) and 'Ginger' Pat Bowman (right). Like Vanda and Pat, Mick Millington and Nick Bernard are seen here also in tracksuits ready to start some sporting competition.

'Big Jack' can be seen at the left of this group of camp staff taking an afternoon off on the Skegness beach. The other staff, clockwise from Jack, are: Cyril Lodge (photographer), Cyril Elliott (organist), Johnny Robins (musician), Harvey Mellors (photographer), Susie (Johnny's wife), Shirley Crook (finance), Eric ? (projectionist), Nora Lodge (Cyril's wife), Pat Bowman (entertainer), Jean Ellis (secretary to General Manager), and the boy is Cyril and Nora's son John Lodge.

'Every morning through my kitchen window I could hear the artistes rehearsing backstage: Roy Tipper ('Mr Theatre'), Bud Bennet the comedian from Blackpool and Mrs Smith's Four Little Boys. I knew most of their routines and catch phrases by heart. "Hello, hello, hello, hello – we are Mr and Mrs Smith's four little boys," they used to sing!'

Margaret Lyon of Skegness – her house on Seathorne Crescent used to back on to the stage door of the camp theatre.

'Mrs Smith's four little boys' on stage at the camp. The young girl to the right is Georgina Millington. As well as entertaining professionally, one of the brothers – Alf Smith – ran the Rose of England pub on Mansfield Road in Nottingham.

HELLO   HELLO!   HELLO!!   HELLO!!!

MRS. SMITH'S FOUR LITTLE BOYS

THE FOUR SMITH BROTHERS

ALF   HAROLD

ROY   STAN

THE FOUR SMITH BROTHERS
IN
"SPECIAL HOLIDAY EXPRESS"
Sunday at 6 p.m. and 8 p.m.

It's not surprising that Mrs Lyon remembers hearing Roy Tipper from her kitchen window on Seathorne Crescent. Roy was the stage manager at the camp for many years and was responsible for pulling the performances together. In this picture Roy is on the right with his wife Myrtle and the camp's organist Cyril Elliott.

'Cyril Elliott — musical director — was the first organist to play the magnificent Compton Organ which was installed for the opening of the new theatre complex after the great fire. Cyril was an excellent organist, well known from the London cinemas and theatres.'

Shirley Crook, now Shirley Mellors.

Debonair Cyril Elliott poses in front of the Compton organ. This mighty music machine was also a favourite setting for taking snapshots of the campers, especially the children, as this brief compilation shows.

In the top right photograph is Christine Burns, daughter of Sally and Harry Burns of Heanor, and in the picture opposite is Melvyn Truswell from Pilsley. Above are Melvin and Eileen Robinson whose father, John William Robinson, worked at Markham pit.

'I had a great year on stage at the Skegness Miners' Camp in 1963. Mainly I played guitar and sang – they called me the yodelling guitarist – but I did a lot of comedy work there as well, with people like Tony Melody and Harry Rolley. You just got stuck in – they were great times!'

Eric Martin, real name Eric Taylor, of Derby.

Eric Martin from Derby – real name Eric Taylor – was a well-known singer and guitarist in the 1950s and 1960s who played in many of the big dance halls and clubs of the time, including the legendary 3Is Club in London. Eric has a natural singing voice and as a boy he sang solo in the leading Derby church choirs. Later, in the RAF, Eric formed his own skiffle group seen opposite performing in Hucknall Miners' Welfare. He went on to a professional singing career and completed a season at the camp in 1963.

This agency publicity shot shows Eric in his main role as singer and guitarist.

However, as this picture shows, Eric was also able to turn his hand to comedy. Here he is second from the right, on stage at the camp with Tony Melody – later well-known as a radio and television personality– taking part in the 'army sketch'.

'Appearing at the Centre this season is the talented comedian George E. Beck. George, whose own father was a miner, started his career as a boy soprano, he toured all the leading theatres, and was chosen to appear before Royalty at the Queen's Hall, London, at the age of 12. His biggest achievement no doubt is that he is the original understudy to the late Arthur Lucan (Old Mother Riley) and he played the part many times on tour.'

Camp Entertainment Programme 1958 season.

Anyone who went to the cinema, or watched TV, in the 1950s will remember those grainy black and white British comedies about 'Old Mother Riley'. George Beck's main claim to fame was as Old Mother Riley's understudy and he can be seen in this role above. However, like many of the performers of his day, George had many talents, including a wonderful singing voice, and he was also a very popular figure at the camp.

George is more than happy to pose with young Sally Burns of Heanor in 1958.

'Little Jackie Wright was on the entertainment staff for many years and later he was to be seen on television as Benny Hill's side kick. He was also a very close friend to Benny. At the camp his main role was in the band playing trumpet and trombone. When the band wasn't playing in the theatre they were playing in the bar and Jackie took great delight when I walked into the bar with Harvey (Harvey Mellors my husband-to-be) of stopping the band and striking up with 'They try to tell us we're too young' as I was only 16 and Harvey was 22! Jackie was always pulling someone's leg. He never married but doted on his sister back home in Belfast.'

Shirley Crook now Shirley Mellors.

As a young boy watching the early Benny Hill shows on the television, I used to think his sidekick, Jackie Wright, was some old 'geezer' who Benny had dragged in off the street. I didn't realise that it was the same accomplished comic and musician who had entertained so many at the camp, nor did I appreciate just how much skill and experience was concealed beneath Jackie's role as Benny's side-kick. As the story above from Shirley Mellors shows, Jackie was a very likeable and very funny man. In the photograph above he poses on stage at the camp, and opposite he can be seen leading the children's parade at the finish of the weekly children's party.

'We had some top-class entertainers during the season. One year Mike and Bernie Winters were regular weekend visitors, as Bernie was 'courting' – and later married – one of our dancers, Ziggy Heine. Mike and Bernie were a great asset, and worked very hard, being involved with the entertainment of the campers during the day and also joining the Shows in the evenings.'

Jean Ellis, now Adams, secretary to J. D. Williamson, General Manager.

Unfortunately, I have not been able to find a photograph of Mike and Bernie Winters at the camp. However, this compilation does show a number of other big names who appeared at the camp. Top left is Mick Millington with jazz musician Kenny ball, whilst Tommy Cooper, above, requires no introduction. Opposite, standing to the left of Mick Millington, is the film and TV comedian Lance Percival.

'Brian the Singing Miner used to bring the house down when he sang at the camp. He had a bad accident at Markham pit that left him unconscious for a while and it was afterwards that his singing career took off. He started singing for his mates in the pit baths and he ended up winning talent competitions at the camp. He was very well known at the time and he used to appear in the pubs and clubs with his backing group The Flying Pit Props – he even made a record. He still sings locally.'

Harry Morris, of Poolsbrook, who worked mainly at Ireland pit.

As part of the research for this book I had the privilege of a great evening with Brian and fellow singer, Vondra Redfern, at the Goldminers pub in Chesterfield. As well as some truly wonderful performances from Vondra, her husband, daughter, son-in-law, and friends, I shall never forget Brian's unique rendition of numbers such as *Green Door, You'll Never Walk Alone* and, of course, *Spanish Eyes.*

Above, left: Brian Ashley the Singing Miner in action in the pubs of Chesterfield. As Harry Morris recalls above, Brian's career as a performer started after his accident when a pit prop flew out under pressure knocking him unconscious. He began his singing in the pithead baths and his career culminated in releasing a record – a cover version of *Spanish Eyes* – with his backing group the Flying Pit Props.

Brian is seen posing with another local singer and friend, Vondra Redfern (left). Vondra, from Newbold Moor Chesterfield, is the daughter of a Derbyshire miner and she also has fond memories of holidaying at the camp. She tells me that she remembers singing on stage at Skegness as a child as part of one of the many children's talent competitions compered by Mick Millington.

'Later on, in the 1960s, the Butterfly cabaret bar was developed and we got some really big names appearing there. Mick used to meet them and make them feel at home – he loved that. I remember Tommy Cooper, Cy Grant, Eddie Calvert, Rosemary Squires and many more.'

Avis Millington.

Top left and right: Tommy Cooper and Cy Grant relaxing at the camp with the Butterfly Ballroom girls; bottom left: trumpet player Eddie Calvert with Mick in the foyer to the ballroom; bottom right: Donald Peers in action in the Butterfly Ballroom.

'As well as the top performers there were always the regular entertainment staff to put on a good show. We usually had a panto with all the regulars on like the Janice Sutton dancers and we usually entered a float in the Skegness carnival.'

Avis Millington.

A British Rail lorry is commandeered for the Derbyshire Miners' Holiday Camp entry for the Skegness carnival in the early 1960s.

A Robin Hood panto with most of the regular entertainment staff on stage including Mick Millington, Nick Bernard and the Janice Sutton dancers.

The Other Staff

A personal message from the General Manager to the campers in the 1950 camp programme.

PERSONAL LETTER TO YOU
from
THE MANAGER

Dear Friends,

On behalf of the Staff and myself, I take this opportunity to welcome you to Skegness.

I can assure you that it is our intention to do everything possible for your comfort, and to enable you to have a memorable holiday.

It is indeed unfortunate that you have not, as yet, gained the two weeks' holiday, however there surely can be no doubt that the time will come (in the very near future, I hope) when this important point of the Miner's Charter is gained.

It is appreciated that during your one week's holiday everything must be done to make the most of every minute of your leisure, and to this end we have compiled a full entertainment programme, for young and old alike.

The parents who wish to leave their children in capable hands, whilst they themselves have a few hours of freedom may do so with confidence. Further details of this service will be found elsewhere in this programme.

In conclusion, I should like to invite two or three ladies to join the weekly Committee which we form from among the Campers, and they can then speak on behalf of the womenfolk.

I hope the weather will be fine, and that your holiday will be fully satisfactory. I can assure you, that you will receive service with courtesy, from the whole staff. Should you have any complaints or suggestions to make, please let me know, when every consideration will be given to them.

Yours sincerely,

J. D. WILLIAMSON.

The staff line-up from the 1964 camp programme.

'When I was a kid your family had about as much chance of owning a camera as you did your own car. In those days the only photos you had were when you went to a wedding, or when the photoman came round at camp.'

Dave Eyley of Blackwell.

Cyril Lodge collapses after an exhausting day behind the camera. Cyril, originally from Nottingham, was the camp's first official photographer and was later joined by Harvey Mellors and Peter Nolan. I understand the 'photographic services' badge on Cyril's blazer was smuggled out of the neighbouring Billy Butlin's camp.

In the bottom right of the photograph, is the kiosk from which the photographic department would display and sell the snaps taken the previous day. Also in this picture can be seen union leader, Bert Wynn, talking to a group of men, and strolling across with newspaper in hand is Johnny the musician!

'Peter Nolan and my husband-to-be Harvey Mellors took over the running of the camp's photographic department from Cyril Lodge. Peter was mainly behind the camera and Harvey looked after the darkroom. They had a staff of four, including the assistant in the kiosk selling the photographs. Friday night was carnival night and it went on till after midnight. The photographs taken during the evening had to be developed, printed and on sale by 8 o'clock the next morning so it was all hands to the deck with the staff working through the night.'

Shirley Crook, now Shirley Mellors.

Harvey Mellors, left, and Peter Nolan, right, lark about with one of their photographic tricks. Harvey and Peter ran the camp's photographic department after taking over from its founder Cyril Lodge in the early 1950s. It was Shirley's husband to be, Harvey Mellors, who tended to look after the darkroom side of the operation, see below, whilst Peter was usually out and about in the camp taking the pictures.

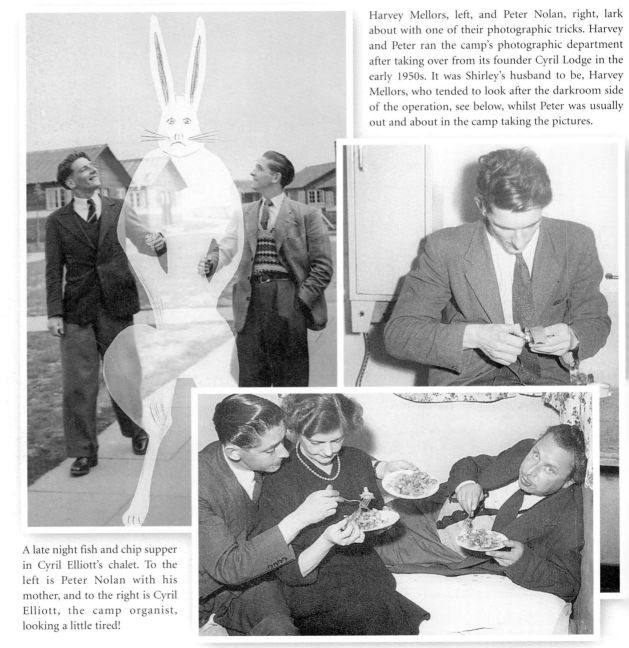

A late night fish and chip supper in Cyril Elliott's chalet. To the left is Peter Nolan with his mother, and to the right is Cyril Elliott, the camp organist, looking a little tired!

'My mam and dad met at the camp when they were both working there. Dad was a bit of a lad and someone bet him that he couldn't get a date with each week's Ideal Holiday Girl. He won the bet but I'm not sure what happened at the end of the season when all the girls came together for the finals! Mam and dad obviously had the time of their lives working at the camp and they used to love watching Hi di Hi on TV and reminiscing about their time at the Derbyshire Miners'.'

Mary Nolan, now Mary Whetstone of Mansfield. Mary's father was Peter Nolan, camp photographer, and her mother Margaret was a nurse who worked at the camp caring for the paraplegic miners.

Peter Nolan, described in a camp programme as: 'Our handsome roving cameraman whose duty and pleasure is to capture in camera those fleeting moments of holiday happiness and preserve them in film.' Talking to people who knew Peter it is true he was very much at home behind the camera, mixing with the campers and capturing them on film at their best and funniest.

Indeed, as these two photographs opposite clearly show, Peter was more than capable of having a bit of a laugh himself. Top right: Peter nursing one of his little babies at the engagement party of Harvey Mellors and Shirley Crook! Bottom right: Peter raises his profile with organist Cyril Elliott in front of the paraplegic block, still under construction in this photograph.

'An appeal has been launched by a Derbyshire family to revive memories of the The Derbyshire Miners' Holiday Camp. Many of the family's old photographs of the camp have this stamped on the back: 'Souvenirs by Frank Richards, 42 Seathorne Crescent, Skegness'. Does anyone remember Frank? Do any of his relatives still live in the Skegness area?'

Skegness newspaper article.

My newspaper appeal was answered by Frank Richards' daughter, Margaret Gorringe, who now lives in Northampton. Above, Frank Richards' photographic shop in the 1950s on Seathorne Crescent at the back of the camp. Frank, seen opposite on location with his camera and flashgun, was not a member of the camp staff but he was well known to many of the campers and so I thought it appropriate to include him in this section. Frank was an electrician by trade and he was obviously a clever and enterprising chap, as the pages which follow demonstrate.

'A friend in Skegness said someone was trying to find 'Frank Richards' the photographer. Well, I'm Frank's daughter. Our name is really Grebby but the photographic shop Dad bought near the camp was called 'Frank Richards', so he just kept the name. He did all the developing at the back of the shop and I remember the smell of the chemicals. Dad used to store the stuff in lemonade bottles and I was always being warned not to drink out of them! I remember the house was always full with all sorts of people popping in, musicians and entertainers. For me and my little sister it was a great time.'

Margaret Grebby, now Margaret Gorringe, of Northampton.

'Frank Richards' in the gorilla suit at the wheel of his car. Both the gorilla suit and the sports car were two of Frank's many trademarks to catch the public eye and provide a snapshot with that extra bit of interest. As a child growing up in a busy, creative household, Margaret remembers all sorts of colourful characters – comedians and musicians – popping in, often late into the night. Standing behind the car in this picture Margaret remembers, from left to right, a harpist, drummer, a red-haired Irish accordionist and trumpet player.

The assistant – another red-haired woman – employed by Frank to look after the shop on Seathorne Crescent. At the back of the shop on display are some of the snaps still waiting to be collected by holidaymakers.

'Dad was always inventing novel ways of getting people to have their photo taken. He made a big wooden television set you sat in to make it look like you were on tele, and then there was the big board you stuck your head through to make it look like you were wearing a bikini! And of course, there were his Polar Bear and Gorilla outfits!'

Margaret Gorringe of Northampton.

Some of Frank's little tricks of the trade. Clockwise from above, the Polar Bear out and about in the pubs of Skegness; Frank's daughter Margaret and her younger sister on the horse in front of the shop; Frank and friends 'inside' his TV; Norman Gration and Arthur Brown behind the 'bikini board' which also stood outside the shop.

'*In the early 1950s I worked at the camp in the finance department as assistant to Cliff Cameron, the camp's accountant. In 1953 I was fortunate enough to win the 'Ideal Staff Girl' silver cup donated by Fred Smith, a miner of Porterhouse Road Ripley, in memory of his late wife. Their daughter Kathleen Smith also worked at the camp one season.*'

Shirley Crook, now Shirley Mellors.

Shirley Crook being presented with the 'Ideal Staff Girl' cup in 1953. Standing either side of Shirley are her boss, the camp's accountant Cliff Cameron, and his wife Alice. Shirley remembers that the cup was donated by miner Fred Smith in memory of his late wife. She can even remember Fred's address – Porterhouse Road, Ripley! I am unsure for how many years after 1953 the title of 'Ideal Staff Girl' was awarded.

Kathleen Smith, daughter of Fred Smith who introduced the 'Ideal Staff Girl' cup in memory of his late wife. Like many members of Derbyshire mining families, Kathleen worked at the camp for a while.

'It was a good life working at the camp. The General Manager, Jack Dennis Williamson – J. D. as we all called the boss – never bothered anyone. As long as he knew everything was going as it should, he was happy. There was no clocking on and off – if you finished your work you went off duty and by the same token you stayed behind if something needed doing.

Shirley Crook, now Shirley Mellors.

In the centre of the front row is Jack Dennis Williamson – better known as 'J. D.' – the camp's longest serving General Manager. 'J. D.' joined the camp in the 1940s and, according to a report in the *Derbyshire Times*, formerly worked at the Miners' Hostel in Alfreton, Derbyshire. In this photograph from the late 1940s, standing from the left, are: Mick Millington, George Worsley (Head Chef), Winston Wood (Cashier), Bill Maw (Musician), Jim Crosby (Head Waiter). Seated from the left, are: Ivy Staley (Head Housekeeper), Mr Bennett (Catering Manager), J. D. Williamson, Cliff Cameron (Accountant), Cyril Lodge (Photographer).

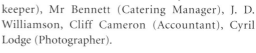

In this real live action picture, J.D. is seeing off a couple of 'spivs' who have strayed into the camp to ply their trade. Harvey Mellors, ex-camp photographer, tells me that this kind of problem happened from time to time and that the children's entertainer, 'Big Jack' Simpson, was usually called upon to lend a hand.

'I was working as a waiter at the camp in 1949 when I met my wife there. We had a wonderful time. Wish we were doing it now. All my brothers, father and brothers-in-law, and myself worked down the mines till they closed. Many people from mining families used to work at the camp.

Mr A. E. Smith of Stonebroom.

Top: Far left is Mr Smith at the camp in 1949 with other members of the catering staff. Note the cigarette tucked behind the ear of the chap on the right, Johnny Jackson, who later joined the entertainment staff!

Middle: This photograph of the wedding of two camp staff shows Doreen Walters, now Brooker, fifth from the right. Doreen's father, Jack Walters, worked at Pilsley pit for many years. Doreen was working at the camp as a waitress when she met her friend Carrie who in the picture has just married Bill, a chef at the camp. Standing at the back, to the right-hand side of the doorway, is J. D. Williamson and his wife. Camp musician Bert Patchett Senior, and his wife, are standing to the right of the group.

Left: This group photograph of catering staff was taken in the 1950s in the new theatre. Second and third from the right are Don McPherson and Joan Clarke who later married. Joan's father was Ripley miner Doug Clarke.

'Lots of the staff were related and many came from mining families. One season there were seven from one family working at the camp. Doris Eames (head housekeeper), her husband Fred (maintenance), her sister Dora McGowan (children's dormitory matron), Dora's husband Alf (maintenance), Doris and Dora's brother George Wilkinson (maintenance and bar), George's wife Dot (children's dormitory) and for one summer George's father. As well as the Eames family, I remember 'one leg Bob', Bob Southern. He was in charge of 'veg prep' and was often seen sitting outside peeling potatoes, a cigarette in his mouth. Imagine doing that by hand for around a thousand people every day, sometimes twice a day if potatoes were to be used for both main meals.'

Shirley Crook, now Shirley Mellors.

From the right, Mick Millington with 'one leg' Bob Southern (veg prep), Bert Patchett Snr (musician), Doris and Fred Eames (housekeeper and maintenance), Harvey Mellors (photographer), Sid Wade (bar). Shirley and Harvey Mellors, who made this picture available, were not able to identify the woman at far left.

A line of laundry staff. Len Gage and Pat Tyler are first and second from the left, Ken Smith and Cath Lightfoot are first and second from the right. Unfortunately, I am not able to identify the three middle women.

'I was the secretary to the camp's General Manager, J. D. Williamson, or 'J. D.' as he was generally known. I used to deal with all the bookings and the allocation of accommodation. Saturdays were always quite a day, with people coming back year after year and often asking for the same chalets, and for the same 'neighbours'! It was great to welcome back so many people who seemed like old friends, sharing some of their joys and sorrows – I remember the bad time after the Creswell Colliery disaster when 80 men had died underground!'

Jean Ellis, now Adams.

Jean Ellis with other staff in front of the camp's main reception. From the left: Bert Patchett Snr (trumpet player), Harvey Mellors (photographer), Don Statham (camp shop manager), Jean Ellis (general manager's secretary), Nora Faunt (camp office and wife of Bernard Faunt, better known as Nick Bernard, camp entertainer), Alec Lakin (assistant catering manager), Eric Stroud (pianist and entertainer).

The staff from the camp shops pose near the chalet that was used by the photographic department for developing film. As you can see, false nose and moustache sets were a popular novelty item that year!

The 'Con Home', 'Para Block' & 'The St John's'

'Some years ago I went to visit a mate of mine in hospital in Derby. In the next bed there was an old miner I knew from way back from Stanley Village. He kept asking me how he could get down to the beach. Years before he'd spent some time in the Convalescent Home at Skegness. Poor old lad thought he was back in Skeg.'

Alan Cooper of West Hallam.

The 'Con Home', as it was always called by the miners, was built by the Derbyshire Miners' Association in 1928 and prior to that the union provided convalescence in rented accommodation in Skegness. This 1960s photograph shows the front of this magnificent building directly overlooking the sea.

This photograph, also taken in the 1960s, shows the side of the Con Home from Winthorpe Avenue and when considered together with the view above demonstrates the sheer size of the building.

'When I was 17 or 18 I had over a year in and out of hospital and then at the end I had 3 weeks in the Con Home at Skegness. It must have been 1936 or 1937. I'd been working underground, knee deep in water for months, and I got pleurisy and pneumonia. I got septicaemia and they thought I'd died. I must have been off work for the best part of 2 years – no wages and not a penny of compensation.'

Jim Leighton, Alfreton Pit.

The Con Home not only provided convalescence for working miners but also for retired miners and the relatives of mining families. This photograph shows the Con Home's manager, Mr Clayton, surrounded by female relatives of Derbyshire mining families who were convalescing at Skegness in 1936. My aunt Doris who was recovering from a kidney infection at the time is at bottom right. She befriended the woman top left who was terminally ill with cancer and who died soon after. I understand that Johnny Clayton never married, devoting his life to the running of the home from the early 1930s until he retired.

This photograph, taken in front of the main entrance, shows a gathering of miners and ex-miners of all ages complete with moustaches, waistcoats, gold watch chains and slippers! It was loaned to me by John Caulton of Ripley whose father Steve Caulton was active in the Derbyshire Miners' Association and can be seen on the next to the back row, tenth from the right.

'We're still providing a good service to miners, nearly all of them in retirement now, and to miners' widows and other relatives. As you can see, people from the mining communities still come here and enjoy their break. We've got some excellent accommodation here, better than many good hotels, and although some of the rooms are still moth-balled we would like to open up our facilities to a wider audience.'

John Brown, General Manager of the Derbyshire Miners' Convalescent Home

This compilation of photographs shows the Con Home as it is today run by the Coal Industries Social Welfare Organisation (CISWO) under the general managership of Mr John Brown.

A huge banner above the main doorway proudly proclaims that this is the 'Derbyshire Miners' Convalescent Home', still in operation and still a credit to its founding fathers.

Through the main entrance and into the spacious foyer. The Con Home is in an excellent state of repair and many of the original fixtures and fittings survive, including the oak panelling.

The magnificent billiards room overlooking the seafront.

Mrs Leverton and Mrs Riley relax in the afternoon in the ballroom, once the site of the camp's Butterfly Ballroom and the venue of many famous cabaret performances including those of Tommy Cooper, Kenny Ball, Donald Peers and others. Mrs Leverton and Mrs Riley are from Mansfield Woodhouse and are the widows of Nottinghamshire miners.

'I used to be invited to the Paraplegic Block on Friday evenings to take photographs. They were never miserable, the 'paraplonks', as they called themselves. They always seemed to be larking about. They'd grab hold of your hand and start wrestling with you. You couldn't get away because of the strength in their arms.'

Harvey Mellors, Camp photographer.

The first Paraplegic Block, above, was built in the early 1950s between the holiday camp and the Con Home, a part of which can be seen in the top left-hand corner of this photograph. The Para Block, as it was called, was eventually replaced with more up-to-date facilities in the 1970s.

Camp photographer, Harvey Mellors, remembers the Para Block with affection and respect and this picture of paraplegic miners enjoying the sun was produced by him in 1952 or 1953.

'I'd only met Gary just a couple of months before his accident underground, so you see, most of our courtship was in the hospital!'

Freda, wife of paraplegic miner Gary Cooper.

This picture of Gary Cooper and his wife Freda was taken at the camp not long after his accident at Swanwick pit in 1956 at the age of 21.

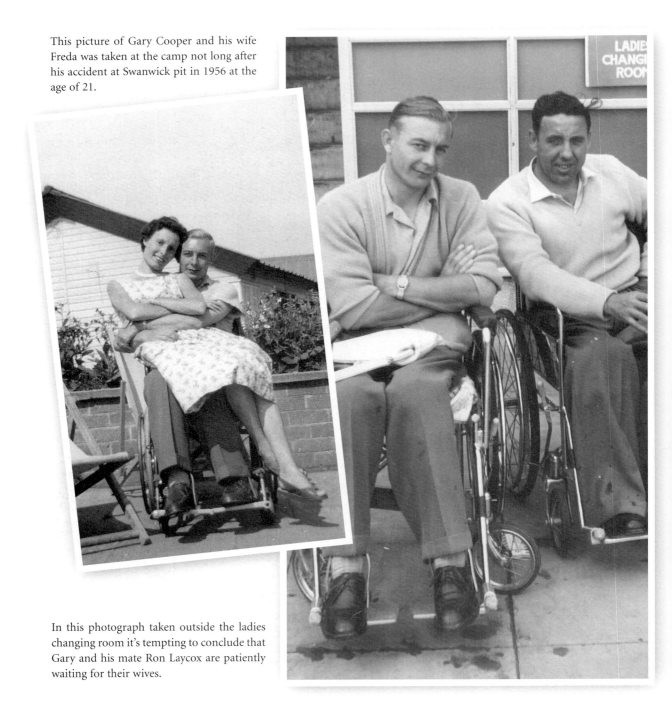

In this photograph taken outside the ladies changing room it's tempting to conclude that Gary and his mate Ron Laycox are patiently waiting for their wives.

'We were always having a bit of a laugh and a joke in the Para Block. It was everybody else who seemed so serious. One time I remember this fella from a local newspaper came to the Para Block to talk to me and my two mates. He asked us our names so I said, "I'm Gary Cooper". My mate said, "I'm Tommy Cooper" and my other mate said, "I'm Bing Crosby". Well, he wasn't very pleased – he thought we were pulling his leg, so he went to one of the paraplegic nurses to complain but she said: "It's true, he is called Gary Cooper, and he's called Tommy Cooper and the other one's George Crosby but everybody calls him 'Bing'!"'

Gary Cooper.

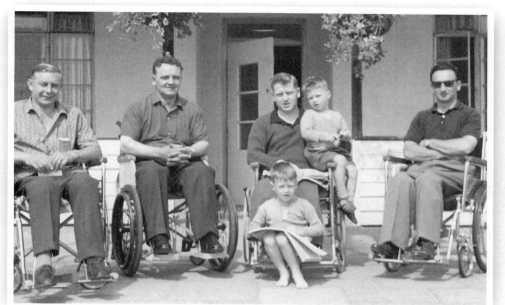

Here's Gary Cooper with three of his mates in front of the Para Block. Unfortunately, Tommy Cooper and 'Bing' Crosby didn't make it into this photograph! From left to right are Gary Cooper, Alf Lowe, Dennis Curley and David Sasic.

In the gardens of the Para Block in 1963. At the front, from left to right are Clarence Priestley, Alf Lowe, Gary Cooper, Freda Cooper, and Doris and Len Glen with the children. Further along are David Sasic and Mr Buxton.

'In a lot of the photographs in the Para Block you can see us standing up holding on to something. You see, when you're on your backside for so long you can get a bit numb and you can get like bed sores, so you see you have to give your backside a bit of a break.'

Gary Cooper.

And here is Gary taking a welcome 'backside break' in the Paraplegic Block in the late 1950s.

When the weather was fine, playing dominoes in the gardens of the Para Block was a favourite pastime. Here's Gary again in the centre of the domino group with Len Glen of Loscoe to his right.

'This is me in bed with Pat Phoenix. I used to have a little nap most afternoons when I was staying in the Para Block and one time there was a knock on the door and in walks Pat Phoenix. I didn't even have time to comb my hair so I just pushed it back off my face and put my arm round her.'

Len Glen, paraplegic miner, Ormonde pit.

Len Glen is pictured here with Pat Phoenix of *Coronation Street* fame when she visited the paraplegic block in 1966 and made an impromptu call to his bedroom! Pat signed autographs that day which campers could buy as part of a fund-raising campaign.

Right: Another paraplegic miner who regularly visited the camp was Vin Doggart of Langley Mill. Len Glen remembers Vin as quite a character and like the other paraplegic miners was more than capable of enjoying himself, whatever the occasion and whatever the circumstances. This picture from 1960 shows Vin and his wife with Len's wife Doris at the back. To the right is Doris's sister Betty Glen who was married Len's brother.

'There used to be a lot of us around just a few years ago. Every year there used to be a Christmas do for paraplegics and their wives in one of the big Miners' Welfares. I can remember when there were more than 8 paraplegic miners just around Heanor. We used to see a lot of each other but there's not many of us left now.'

Len Glen.

This particular annual Christmas 'do' for the paraplegic miners of Derbyshire is from the mid-1960s and was held, I believe, in the Miners' Welfare on Nottingham Road in Ripley. Len Glen and Gary Cooper are sitting next to each other, with their wives, towards the centre of the middle row.

Gary Cooper relaxes in the gardens of the paraplegic block in the early 1970s.

'I remember being at the camp in the same year when the great East Coast floods nearly ruined the place. It was 1953 I think; that would be five years before I had my accident at Ormonde pit.'

Len Glen.

1953, the year of the great East Coast floods. Standing at the right of the group is Len Glen. The man with the pint pot raised to his mouth is Keith Harvey, and in front of him is Orton Sims, both of whom worked at Ormonde pit with Len.

Len Glen in 1961 coming up Winthorpe Avenue towards the camp with his wife Doris and two of his children, Lynne and Kenny.

'There was a group of Notts paraplegic miners who got their 'compen' round about the same time so they bought houses on the same street. The locals called it 'Para Row'.'

Gary Cooper.

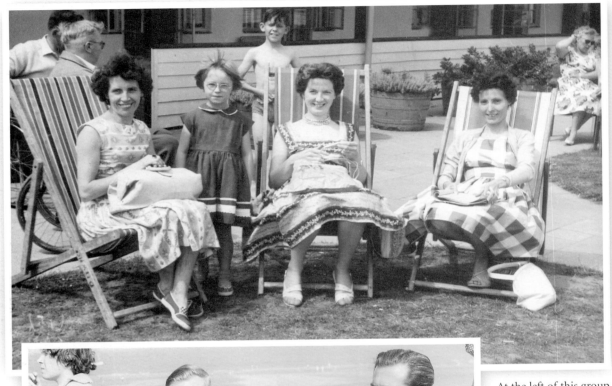

At the left of this group above is the wife of one of the six Nottinghamshire miners living on 'Para Row', Reg Polak from Calverton. In the middle is Sheila Johnson, wife of Kenny Johnson, and to the right is Freda Cooper.

Enjoying an ice cream with Gary Cooper is Kenny Johnson to the right of the picture. Before his accident Kenny worked at Ormonde pit and tragically he died before reaching his 40th birthday.

'When the pits closed the St John's Ambulance Brigade collapsed in North Derbyshire. Before then lots of people from mining families – boys and girls – were involved in the Brigade. Sometimes I was out nearly every night teaching first aid. We had barn dances and galas organised by the Brigade, and of course all of the Derbyshire St John's people used to go for a special weekend at the miners' camp at the end of every season.'

Rex Darricott, from Duckmanton near Chesterfield. Rex worked all his life in the pits, starting at 14 as a 'pick boy' and pony lad, finishing at the Markham pits as Assistant Safety Officer. Rex was also Markham Divisional Superintendent in the St John's Ambulance Brigade.

Nursing Cadets of the Bolsover Division of the St John's Ambulance Brigade in front of the children's dormitory at the camp in the 1960s. Standing next to the Divisional shield is Supt. Mrs West.

Nursing Cadets of the Ireland Division in front of the Con Home at camp in 1951. Standing at the left of picture are: Mrs May Ward, Mrs June Tuffs and Mrs Anna Rodd. Standing at the right is Mrs Kathleen Staniland, and standing second from the right is Miss Bingham who I believe is now the head of the baby unit at Chesterfield Hospital.

'My father – Jack Wrigley – was an ambulance driver at Renishaw Park pit. Dad was also a member of the St John's Ambulance Brigade and every year they went for a long weekend at the camp where they paraded down Winthorpe Avenue after Church.'

Janet Wrigley, now Janet Wright of Spinkhill, near Chesterfield.

Derbyshire St John's Ambulance Brigade members take the salute in Skegness on their parade back to the miners' camp after the traditional Sunday church service. Janet Wright's father – Jack Wrigley – is towards the front of the first line.

Nurses and nursing cadets of the Ireland Division of the St John's Ambulance Brigade on their way back through Skegness to the miners' camp. At the front of the parade are: Mrs May Ward, Mrs Anna Rodd, Mrs Kathleen Staniland and Mrs June Tuffs.

'We had some good lads in the St John's in those days, they worked hard and learnt a lot. Many of them would go down the pits but some of them went on to the fire service or police force. The highest award for a cadet was the Grand Prior Award and for that you had to achieve in 12 subjects including first aid, signalling and fire fighting.'

Rex Darricott of Duckmanton, near Chesterfield.

Cadets of the Markham Division of the St John's Ambulance Brigade receiving their Grand Prior Awards at the camp in 1968. Standing at left of picture is Julian Turbiaz and at the right is Alan Burrows. Next to Divisional Supt. Rex Darricott is Barry Jakeman.

Cadets of the Markham Division at the camp winning the flag for the best Division of 1977. From the left: the Lord Lieutenant of Derbyshire Colonel Hilton, Area Staff Officer for cadets Fred Bottom, Sgt. Shaun Bailey, Sgt. Jason Owen and Sgt. Lyndon Tuffs.

'We did used to have some fun on the special weeks at the camp for disabled people. I used to go as a medic and help out with the carers and social workers. We usually finished with a football match and it always ended up in good-humoured chaos with buckets of water and shaving foam!'

Rex Darricott of Duckmanton, near Chesterfield.

One of the football matches at the special weeks at the camp in the late 1980s mentioned above by Rex Darricott. Rex is kneeling at the right of the picture with 'I am kinky' daubed in lipstick across his chest!

A 1987 special holiday week at the camp for the physically disabled. In the background, to the right of the picture, is the paraplegic block which replaced the original facilities built in the early 1950s. Rex Darricott was on hand once again as a medic and he can be seen standing fourth from the right in the second row.

Index